Urban
Wild

Helen Rook

Urban Wild

52 Ways to Find Wildness on Your Doorstep

BLOOMSBURY WILDLIFE
LONDON • OXFORD • NEW YORK • NEW DELHI • SYDNEY

Thank you. You know who you are.

This book is dedicated to my best friend Mia (aka 'The Sniffs'), my partner in urban adventures, whose parting from this world inspired me to write this book and whose company I still miss to this day. I hope we meet again, ginger shadow.

BLOOMSBURY WILDLIFE
Bloomsbury Publishing Plc
50 Bedford Square, London, WC1B 3DP, UK
29 Earlsfort Terrace, Dublin 2, Ireland

BLOOMSBURY, BLOOMSBURY WILDLIFE and the Diana logo are trademarks of
Bloomsbury Publishing Plc

First published in the United Kingdom 2022

A catalogue record for this book is available from the British Library.
Library of Congress Cataloguing-in-Publication data has been applied for.

ISBN: HB: 978-1-4729-9096-9; ePDF: 978-1-4729-9087-7; ePub: 978-1-4729-9088-4

2 4 6 8 10 9 7 5 3 1

Design by Gridlock Design
Printed and bound in China by C&C Offset Printing Co., Ltd.

To find out more about our authors and books visit www.bloomsbury.com
and sign up for our newsletters.

Contents

The planting of the seed

I've always been a nature kid. I grew up in a small market town in West Yorkshire, in a terraced house that backed onto fields that seemed – to me as a child – to go on and on forever. I used to cross the fields every day on my way to school, but I was rarely on time as there was so much to investigate. Luckily for me, my patient mum allowed me the freedom to cultivate the awe and wonder that the natural world inspires. When we were younger, my best friend and I spent most of our days outside, swinging in the gnarled weeping willow down the old tip, building dens in the hedgerows, snouting around for conkers at the local park and standing under cascades of rainwater that poured off the disused mill at the end of my street. As a teenager, I roamed the fields to care for a horse, which I had on free loan from a local one-eyed Romany, meeting up daily with riders of my own age to go down to the river, or up the Chevin (a woodland above my town, which these days they call a country park).

My dad was a teacher, as was my mum before she had us, so we were used to long holidays. We stayed pretty local for the half terms, in places like Hinderwell or Filey on the Yorkshire coast, where I would disappear for hours, returning with a bottle of sticklebacks I'd caught from the pond or pockets full of dead crabs. But my sisters and I most looked forward to the summer; seven or so weeks' camping in Cornwall, a family exodus with an old Ford Cortina packed to the gills with the five of us, our kit and the family cat, who occasionally tried to jump out of the moving vehicle when he caught the smell of the countryside.

My sisters were so embarrassed by the spectacle we must have been that they hid under tea towels in the back seat as we passed through town, not realising that they were only adding to the performance for any onlookers. Once, on the journey down, our tent blew off the roof rack on the M1. In a mild panic, Dad pulled onto the hard shoulder and chased it down the motorway. Things were a little different back then.

When we finally arrived, we had weeks of freedom, sleeping under canvas or sometimes on the beach beneath the stars. We witnessed massive thunderstorms, where Dad would scoop us out of our tents, still tucked up in our sleeping bags, and put us in the car for safety until the worst had passed; floods, which created water beds under our roll mats; and heatwaves, weather we rarely saw in Yorkshire, where you could not stay still on the sand for too long or the soles of your feet would burn. I spent most of my time in the sea, hours just floating around on my battered, polystyrene surfboard with my holiday mates, whom we met up with every year. One of the highlights for all of us was waiting for a low, low tide so that the water in front of the 'island' just offshore, which you could only reach under certain tidal conditions, would turn into a lagoon that we could wade across to jump off the island's ledges and sniff around in its rock pools. Our parents were around somewhere, but we had the freedom to roam and to explore.

A 2007 study for the RSPB by Dr William Bird showed how restricted our experiences of nature have become in just a few decades. This research was demonstrated in a study the same year into the roaming distances of eight-year-olds from the same family over four generations. In 1926, when George Thomas was eight

(aged 88 at the time of research and the great-granddad of the family), he walked 6 miles to his favourite fishing spot without supervision. By 1950, George's son-in-law Jack Hattersley, now 63, had roamed just 1 mile to local woods. In 1979, George's granddaughter Vicky Grant, now 36, had roamed a comparatively tiny half mile, and by 2007, George's great-grandson Edward, who is driven to school, taken to a safe place to ride his bike and whose friends play indoors, roams no more than 300 yards. That's 0.27km or 0.17 miles, which is around 400 adult steps. I had a lucky childhood.

I never expected that, as an adult, I would buy my first house in the inner city; I'm really not sure how that happened. Available finances and work, I guess, but here I am. In 2016, like me, 82.84 per cent of the UK's population were reported to live in urban areas – that's about 54 million people – and across the globe, the number was around 55 per cent and rising steadily. There is no surprise that 60 per cent of these urban dwellers are under the age of 45; people need to be able to earn a living.

For me, that is teaching art and outdoor studies with young people who have been failed by our education system, who have been told 'we don't care if you are a fantastic dancer, painter or even scientist; if you don't pass your maths and English, you are not worthy'. Each year in September, the stories I hear break my heart. Every year, I feel privileged to work with such bright, young sparks and to see them flourish as they begin to see that who they are is enough, that they are interesting, and that it is OK not to be 'perfect'.

I work in one of the most deprived areas of the British Isles, where this urban living has come at a cost. Recent air quality maps of the UK (see Resources, p. 220) show almost 2,000 areas, the majority of which are largely urban, where pollution levels are higher than recognised safety limits. That means 94.6 per cent of the UK's population is breathing air that doesn't meet World Health Organisation (WHO) guidelines, with pollution-related illness at a record high. Alongside that, the number of clinically obese people in this country has tripled between 1975 and 2016, and WHO has rated physical inactivity as one of the major contributory factors in early mortality in the developed world, with a recent report from the Chief Medical Officer estimating annual costs in England of £8.2 billion. It's not just our physical health that has suffered from our nature disconnect, the same research found that people deprived of contact with nature are at a higher risk of depression and anxiety, among a plethora of other things.

To combat the stressors of the modern world, people more and more are looking back to nature. I find my sanctuary on my urban allotment (shown on p. 9 and p. 11), where I compete with the slugs, snails, mice and weather to grow just a little organic veg and buckets full of cut flowers. Many of us are becoming increasingly aware of the problems we are facing within our immediate environment. But we can't all simply move to the country; there are too many of us, and we are used to certain privileges that the urban environment brings.

If this all seems a bit gloomy, then do not fret; it is not a hopeless cause. We do have options, ways we can have natural experiences in an urban environment all year round, and with respect for the natural world. This book is a collection of some of those ways that I connect with nature, despite my city home. As I see it, the greening of our cities is something we can all be part of, and finding nature in them is absolutely vital for our survival.

A note on safety

The activities in this book reflect the ebb and flow of the seasons, times with high energy and action interspersed with times to slow down, take stock and reflect on life. There are even some activities for when the weather doesn't tempt you outside. I hope you enjoy, as much as I do, discovering new ways to interact with this beautiful Earth.

Foraging rights have changed over the years, and having once had common land, where our families could play, hunt, gather firewood and such like, we are now expected to ask our local council for permission before we collect anything from our surroundings. However, most councils have bigger issues to deal with and do not object to you foraging safely.

- Make sure you can properly identify what you are collecting. There are many edibles around but there are also some deadly plants that you need to be aware of. If you are unsure, dried herbs can be bought from a variety of sellers (see Resources on p. 220 for links to the Woodland Trusts' seasonal guide to foraging and to G Baldwin & Co., a reputable online source of herbs)

.

- Try to find an area less used by dog walkers. If this is not possible then make sure you are a little way away from the car parks, where most dogs relieve themselves pretty quickly!

- Collect from above knee height, where there is less chance for animal contamination.

- When collecting it is best to do so on a sunny day in the morning, when the useful volatile oils are most active in the plant.

- If you are pregnant, or suffer from an existing ailment, it is best to seek professional medical advice before using wild food and herbs.

- Always choose clothes appropriate for the weather.

- Gather only what you need.

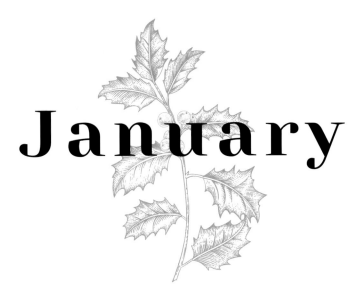

January

January is one of the hardest times of year in the northern hemisphere. Though the shortest day of the year has passed, you don't really see much benefit, especially in the mornings, and the sparkle that gets you through an otherwise dreary December is now packed back into the loft! Not only that but the stores of vitamin D from the long summer days are in short supply in our bodies; we are almost the furthest away from sunshine as we will get during this rotation of the Earth. These days in January are often colder than the ones before Christmas, offering their own variety of doorstep adventures, but if you really can't bear this time of year, at least there is hope. The boldest of spring bulbs are likely to be starting to push through the soil, waking from their silent slumber, hinting towards the promise of shorter nights and warmer days.

This month we will be awakening your senses to the natural world, through sight, sound and smell as you step out into your local environment and meet it properly, perhaps for the first time.

Take a tree shower

Most children, and probably many adults too, are more able to talk to you about what is going on halfway across the world in the rainforests than to tell you anything about their local trees. It's not as hard as you think to identify many native specimens in winter, though it does take a little more attention to detail, and attention to detail is exactly the quality we are intending to cultivate. Forest Bathing is English for *shinrin-yoku*, a practice originating in Japan, which literally translates as 'Forest Shower'. In Japan, a series of studies in 2005 found, through blood and urine tests, that the levels of cortisol (that's the stress hormone, which we are all familiar with) are decreased after spending just two hours in nature. Alongside that, there is growing evidence that nature has a wealth of benefits, from improved cardiovascular health to better cognitive functioning, improved energy to better sleeping patterns and even an increase in the body's natural cancer-killing cells. This concept was recognised in 1984 by scientist Edward Wilson, who formulated the Biophilia hypothesis, that connection with the natural world is an innate, biological need for humans. This is actually so obvious I'm surprised we've had to prove it. Although finding an actual woodland holds more health benefits, you can get started with just one tree.

There will be a huge variety of trees to look at in your local park, and taking the time to really observe them is likely to improve your mood. This is because of the way our brains are wired. When you are not focused on anything, the brain's 'default mode network' steps in; this part of the brain is responsible for ruminating and planning or thinking about the past, among other things. However, when you give your brain something to do, this default setting shuts down, bringing your attention to the moment and some well-deserved relaxation.

Here's how

1 Before you start, write down everything that is on your mind, or take a POMS (Profile of Mood States) questionnaire, which you can find online. Switch off your mobile phone to ensure you will not be disturbed.

2 Now head off to the wooded area of your local park, your local woodland, or even just to the trees on your street. Check out the Woodland Trust's Find Woods webpage (see Resources on p. 220) and if you don't have any nearby, tell your local council you want some, explaining how essential they are to your health.

3 While walking, have a look at the branches. You will notice that there are quite obvious differences in the shape, position and colour of the buds. Perhaps some have seeds, berries or cones; this will all help you to find out what they are. It doesn't matter at this stage if you get it wrong, it's the process that counts, but correct identification does help later if you want to work with the trees to make things.

4 Notice how the different species have different haircuts. Choose one that you like and stand with your back against the trunk; feel the support of the tree at different points along your spine.

5 Notice your feet on the ground and be aware of each part of your body in turn, relaxing them as you go: your ankles, calves, knees, thighs, pelvis, belly, chest, back, all the way up your spine to your shoulder blades, neck, face, chin, lips, cheeks, nose, eyes, eyebrows, forehead and scalp. Remember to breathe; don't force it though, just invite the breath in gently.

6 Look up to the sky through the naked canopy and select a branch to investigate. See if you can follow the branch from trunk to tip, then turn round and follow it back again, marking every fork and fold. You can do this either by following it with your eyes, or walking beneath the branch.

7 Explore the bark; what texture, colour and smell does it have? What tiny worlds exist in its surface? How deep are the fissures in the bark? Be aware of what you notice, of any memories or feelings your investigations generate.

8 When you have spent some time with your new friends, take a moment to write down what you are thinking now, or do another POMS test. Bet your bottom dollar there is less on your mind than before you started!

SUPPLIES
Pen and paper
Clothes appropriate for the weather

Sounds of nature

Did you know that in warm weather you are likely to hear sounds faster than on a cold day? This is because the air molecules are already agitated and vibrating, making the sound waves pass more quickly from one point to another. However in winter, or cold weather, you can often hear sounds that are further away, and they appear louder due to a basic scientific principle called refraction. Simply put, as sound waves pass from the cold air near the ground to the warmer air above, they are bent downwards, making them travel greater distances.

This makes winter a good time to go out and listen to some of your local, natural sounds. Studies have found that even listening to nature can lower blood pressure and reduce that old stress hormone cortisol, so get yourself outside.

Here's how

1 Go to an area with an element of nature near your house. Woodlands are great, but if you don't have one of these close by, you could always use a city park, canal side or even your garden.

2 Get in the right frame of mind by asking yourself to slow down. Bring your awareness of your body into this space.

3 Notice the natural noises around you; the birds, the wind in the trees, the rustling of insects in the leaf litter. See what you can hear to your left, your right, in front of and behind you.

4 If you are walking then move slowly, noticing all the different sounds that come into earshot. See how long you can hear them before they just slip out of range.

5 Notice the sounds that are close to you, and then try to hear the most distant sound you can.

6 Come back to your own breath; breathe in through your nose and out through your mouth, just loudly enough to bring it in to join the sound of the forest, park or playing field.

7 Now you are aware of the background orchestra in your area, you will be more able to recognise a sound that seems out of place. A bird with an unusual call, perhaps, or a distant stretch of water that may be worth investigating.

8 Leave feeling relaxed, refreshed and ready for the next part of your day.

SUPPLIES
Your good self

Landscape navigation

It's a good idea to get out of your normal environment and visit somewhere different from time to time. Being in unfamiliar territory puts you in the now, as your brain is focused on processing the new information of the place, meaning that there is no space for rumination, planning or thinking about that to-do list.

In most British cities it only takes a short bus, train or car ride to find a new natural area to explore; this can be an area inside the city with natural features or open countryside. These environments are good places to practise some natural navigation. On your home turf it's likely that you know the basic cardinal directions (north, south, east and west), but in somewhere new you can test yourself by working it out from the landscape, and in so doing asking your mind to be present and giving yourself time to relax. I always find it pretty pleasing when I get it right but there's no need to beat yourself up if you don't.

Here's how

1 When you arrive at your destination, whether you have chosen to stay in town or go further afield, the first thing you need to do is switch on your senses. Each place is unique in sound, shape and light. Become aware of the noises around you, the natural forms within the landscape and where the light is coming from, and make a note of these things.

2 A good place to begin is with the trees; they hold many clues about direction because their growth has been influenced by it. There are a couple of things you can look out for, most prominent in solitary trees:

- In the northern hemisphere, the warmth and light comes from the south; this means there tend to be more branches to the southward side of a tree and more broken or dead branches on the northward side.

- The prevailing wind in the UK comes from the south-west, leading to bigger and more plentiful roots to the south-west side of a tree.

- Wind coming from the south-west can also lead to the tree having a wind-swept hairdo, if it is exposed enough to the elements.

SUPPLIES
Compass to check your findings (optional)

3 In a built-up environment, another clue you can look for is what direction the satellite dishes are pointing. In the UK, these are all roughly facing south-east, hoping to pick up information from the satellite, which is over Africa.

4 Solar panels are another giveaway. As these are trying to catch as much sunlight energy as possible, they are most likely to be facing south.

5 The sun, when we get it, also holds clues. When it is at its highest point in the sky (at roughly 12:00 noon Greenwich Mean Time and 1:00 p.m. British Summer Time) the sun is directly south.

Take your time to familiarise yourself with different systems. In a city this could be the movement of people, funnelling into the station when the working day is done, probably a little more buoyant than when they flocked out of it earlier that morning. There is often a similar pattern around car parks in country areas. Studies show that most people don't stray more than 100m from their car, so the more people you see, the closer you are likely to be to one of these.

Animals also follow regular patterns of movement, and I often watch the crows, gulls and geese heading towards – or away from – the city park, depending on whether it is evening or morning respectively. This can give you insight into what the nearby environment is like.

Be cautious though. Always remember to distinguish between what you actually know and what you only think to be true. I wouldn't want you to end up in a darker part of town, with no idea of how to get home.

Wild pot-pourri

One of the main healing benefits to being in nature, especially woodlands, is that plants release certain chemicals, known as phytoncides. These are natural oils, which the plant uses for its own health and interspecies communication. Obviously the type of phytoncides in an area depends on what grows there and the prevailing environmental factors too. However, alongside many other benefits, which we will come to, phytoncides also give our human immune systems a boost. Amazing, no?

I'm not suggesting that making some natural pot-pourri can prevent all forms of illness, but I do think it is important to recognise how significant our sense of smell is and how it can contribute to our overall well-being. January is not the most inspiring month to be outdoors, seizing moments when you can, so why not bring some of it indoors to enjoy?

Here's how

1 Go out on a woodland walk. I live in the fifth largest metropolitan district and the thirteenth largest city by population in the UK, and I still have daily access to the woods if I have the time. I can't vouch for your home patch but if you aren't sure where there are woods nearby, try the Woodland Trust website in the list of Resources on p. 220. It's also likely you have a council officer in the parks and landscapes department dedicated to this and they are usually very helpful. If you really have no woodland nearby then local parks can prove a valuable source of inspiration too.

2 Keep your eyes open for any interesting things that have been thrown from the trees by wintery winds. Look out for things like pine, alder, cypress and larch cones, eucalyptus fruits, lichen, bits of interesting bark, conkers, seed heads, pine needles and so on. Make sure you only pick things up from the ground though; as a rule of thumb, if it's still on the tree then it is still needed.

3 When you get home, lay all your finds out to dry.

4 To make up the fragrance, combine the ingredients from your supplies list.

5 Add all your found woodland ingredients to the mix, plus any additional extras you want, like whole nutmeg, cinnamon sticks, star anise or dried citrus slices. Put it all in a sealed container and leave it alone for several weeks.

6 When the scents have infused, display your pot-pourri around your home in decorative bowls and breathe deeply as you walk past it, envisaging the many levels on which it can be of benefit to your health.

7 Take it a tiny step further and use your bowls of natural pot-pourri to remind you to be mindful each time you see or smell them, if just for one minute.

SUPPLIES

Something to collect your finds in

10g orris root powder (found among home brewing/home baking supplies)

¼ tsp. ground allspice

1 tsp. ground cinnamon

2 drops lavender oil

2 drops pine oil

2 drops lemon oil

Whole nutmeg, cinnamon sticks, star anise, dried citrus slices (optional)

February

It's a relief to see the calendar change from January to February. OK, so it's not much of an improvement but we are heading in the right direction. Nights are getting lighter, leaving a little time to play outside after work, and though the mornings are still dragging their heels, at least they are starting to make some effort to join in with the spring fever. By the end of February, welcome snowdrops begin to show their faces and, if you get close enough, will share their delicate scent too – not before time as far as I'm concerned. And towards the end of the month, dog walking after work is no longer challenging if you are lucky enough to share your life with one of these amazing creatures.

This month we will be deepening your connection to your local wild spaces by looking for lessons in nature and being aware of some of the other creatures you share it with, as well as bringing a little more of the wild indoors for a natural home spa.

Micro-pilgrimage

The first week in February sees the pagan festival of Imbolc. This is the time when the green goddess of the Earth is said to return to the land from the underworld, and you can certainly see that in the flora, pushing its way up through the ground. Imbolc is the festival of rebirth and new beginnings, and is a good time to get out on a small pilgrimage to reflect on your hopes and dreams for the coming year.

People have been following pilgrimages for as long as can be remembered, for all kinds of religious or personal reasons, and it is this that defines them; they are not about walking for recreation, they are about travelling in search of wisdom.

Here's how

1 Plan a short walk in your local area, based in as much of the natural world as you can find; this could be in nearby woodland, a city park or even just a series of tree-lined streets in your neighbourhood. It does not need to be long, a couple of miles at the very most. Allow yourself plenty of time so that you can observe as much nature as possible on the way. It's worth noting that all forms of walking have been found to relieve stress, however walking in nature also carries restorative qualities.

2 Part of pilgrimage is in the preparation. Pack some basic things in your rucksack like snacks, drinks, a journal and suitable clothes to meet the needs of the unpredictable February weather.

3 Before you set off, consider something you would like to change in your life, perhaps an old habit you would like to leave behind, or a new project you want to start.

4 When you are ready, put on your boots and step out into the world.

5 While you're out and about, be aware of what messages nature holds for you. Take note of any plant, animal or object that you find interesting and that draws your attention. What does it say to you? Do you notice most the sharp protective thorns on the bare bramble bush and feel like you need a bit of protection yourself right now too? Or can you recognise opportunity for growth in a tree that miraculously grows out of the concrete? Perhaps the sunlight through the branches suggests to you that there is light at the end of the tunnel. What else? Whatever you intuit from the land belongs to you at this time. It is not possible to get it wrong.

6 Be thankful for the knowledge you have gained, no matter how large or small, and return to your home, blessed with wisdom you could not have found if you had stayed at home today.

SUPPLIES
Map or description of your route
Your favourite snacks
Journal and pen (optional)
Weather-appropriate clothing

Valentines for the birds

I don't celebrate Valentine's Day in the traditional sense; to me it's just another way for shops to get you to part with your cash, and being from Yorkshire I have deep pockets and short arms – or so it is said. I always have to smile at the mildly panicked male, rushing to get the last bouquet of roses before heading home to the missus, and have to wonder what he is like the rest of the year. I don't object to a day in celebration of love though, and can't see why it has to be restricted to our own species. After the long winter our birds are in need of a bit of support, so it's a timely opportunity to provide them with some regular meals to propel them into the nesting season. According to the RSPB, February is a good time to listen out for the birds; blue tits in particular are likely to be especially vocal. The males go into full song, proving to their potential mates that they are still fit and healthy after the winter, not dissimilar to the human males rushing around to buy flowers I guess!

Of course, you could just go out and buy a bird feeder, but there is more of a connection with things you have crafted for yourself. So here are a couple of very easy ones you could try.

TEACUP BIRD FEEDER
SUPPLIES
Teacup

String

Lard

Bird seed

Small stick or piece of dowel for perch

Find an old teacup or mug in a charity shop. Mix one part lard with two parts bird seed and heat gently in a saucepan until the fat has melted. Combine the ingredients well, then pour into the teacup or mug. Push a stick in on the side opposite the handle to act as a perch, then allow to cool. When it has completely set, tie some string through the cup handle, and hang your feeder where birds can safely feed from it.

SUET LOG

SUPPLIES

Short log, or piece of scrap timber, 46x46mm width is ideal

Metal eye with screw found in most hardware shops

Drill with 19mm bit

75g suet or vegetable shortening

Unsalted peanut butter

Dried fruit

Bird seed

200g cornmeal

Small sticks or pieces of dowel for perches

Find an old, gnarled log or a piece of scrap timber. Screw a small metal eye onto the narrow part at the top and tie string or wire through the eye so that you can attach it to a tree later. At various places along the length of the log drill some 16mm holes, about 4cm deep. Underneath them drill a smaller hole to push in a stick perch if you wish. Melt 75g plain suet or vegetable shortening in a pan and mix in equal amounts of peanut butter, dried fruit and bird seed. Add 200g cornmeal. Spoon the mixture into the larger holes and allow to set.

Here's how

1   When your creations are complete, choose a place where you go or pass through often, perhaps in your garden or on your balcony, and hang them in a tree, or on railings. Do be aware of cats in urban environments and make sure the feeders are positioned high enough so the birds don't come to any harm.

2   Spend some time watching for the birds that come to your feeders, and don't be dismayed if it takes them a little time to find them. Once they are on the feeding route you will often see them at the same time every day; they will even watch you as you go to re-stock from time to time.

3   Make a note of the types of birds that frequent your feeders; naming things in nature makes them feel more part of your life. Use the RSPB's online Identify a Bird guide to help identify them (see link in Resources on p. 220).

4   Why not have a go at drawing some of the birds? To start with, remember that most birds are teardrop shaped; this helps you to position the various parts. A beautiful consequence of learning to draw things in nature is that it brings you closer to the object of focus.

Animal tracking

In the UK we only get on average 15 days a year where the snow actually settles on the ground, with more sightings the further north you go. Though we'd all like a picture-postcard white Christmas, you are more likely to get a snow day in February than in any other month of the year. According to the Met Office, snow falls for an average of 5.6 days in February, compared to a miserly 3.9 in December (5.3 in January and 4.2 in March).

Looking for animal activity is much easier in the snow. In times gone by, the art of tracking would have been a vital skill for survival – and for some, a highly spiritual practice – but today we can just do it for relaxation and enjoyment.

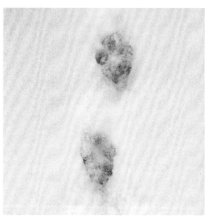

You don't need to wait until it snows; animal tracks can easily be found in mud too, so you just need to get outside and keep your eyes peeled.

Be aware of your own location; there are many different species to be found in urban environments but squirrels are more likely to be in the city centre than stoats, so this can help you narrow down the number of possible suspects for the tracks you see.

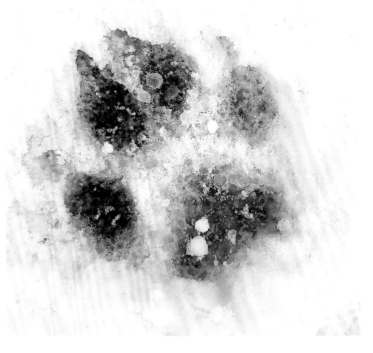

Here's how

1 The first step in identifying an animal print is not to look at the detail but just to note the overall shape. Once you have worked this out, count the toes for more detailed identification.

2 Use the ID table below to identify some of our most common animal tracks.

3 Follow the track for as long as you can, this is often only a few paces.

4 Find a stick which is roughly the length of one of the animal's strides and when the tracks run out, use this stick to see if you can work out where the animal went next by continuing in stick-length increments in the general direction of the tracks until you find prints in the next patch of snow or mud.

5 If you start getting good at this then you can also begin to look at what the tracks are telling you. For example was the animal alone? Are the prints close together or spaced out, indicating whether the animal was trotting or running? Bird prints are especially easy to find in the city, and you can often make out where they landed, where they pecked around for food, where they rested their wings and whether they met a friend. Use your imagination to picture the scene; you will probably find you can pick up more information about the animal than you thought.

SUPPLIES
Photo of the ID table below (optional)

Shape	Toes	Claws visible	Animal	How it looks
Round	4	No	Cat	
Oval	4	Yes	Dog or Fox	Dog Fox
Long, thin oval	5 (hind feet) or 4 (front feet)	Yes	Squirrel	hind foot front foot
Heart-shaped	2	No	Deer	
Square	5	Yes	Badger (4-6cm), Stoat (2cm), Weasel (1.5cm)	
Long and narrow	3 pointing forward with 2 to the side (sometimes only 4 in total are visible)	No	Hedgehog	
Triangle	3, sometimes with another at the back	Yes	Bird	

Home spa facial

With all that outdoor time in wild winter weather, sometimes you just need to warm up. I am so grateful that baths and spas have been invented and can't imagine what life would have been like without them. Civilisations all over the world have valued and ritualised bathing for millennia, so much so that it could be considered part of our evolution. For me, hot baths are a luxury we simply cannot do without! Such a shame that the beauty industry is so damaging to our environment, to our fellow animals and to our own mental health. We need to reclaim self-care and spend some valuable time practising it, at no cost to the Earth.

Here's how

1 Prepare your spa space. All good spas have low lighting, calming music and pleasant aromas drifting on the air. I like candlelight, birdsong and essential oil diffusers.

2 Mix up your face scrub by combining the oatmeal, poppy seeds, sugar and a sprinkle of lavender flowers. Put to one side.

3 Place the rest of the lavender flowers in the heatproof bowl with your chosen essential oils.

4 To first steam your face, place the bowl on a table, fill with boiling water, place your head over the bowl and the towel over your head to catch the vapour. Rest easy for five to ten minutes, breathing more deeply with each breath (it is normal to cough at first). Please be extra careful not to touch the water with your nose or to pull the bowl onto your legs.

5 When you have had enough, rinse your face with cool water.

6 To complete the scrub, mix the dry ingredients you prepared earlier with a little water to form a paste. Apply to your wet face in a gentle circular motion, paying particular attention to your T-zone. Take extra care near your eyes; the skin here is very soft and rarely needs exfoliation.

7 Rinse your face thoroughly, then apply rose water to your cotton pad and use as a toner, making sure to remove the last remnants of the face scrub.

8 When the rose water has dried, finally moisturise as normal.

SUPPLIES

Heatproof bowl and towel

2 tbsp. lavender flowers

Essential oils of your choice. Be careful to choose ones that are safe to inhale. I like thyme and tea tree for their cleansing, antiviral and antibacterial properties.

2 tbsp. coarse oatmeal

1 tbsp. poppy seeds

1 tbsp. sugar

Reusable (preferably) cotton pad

Rose water for use as a toner

March

As the calendar slowly ambles into the month of March and towards spring in the northern hemisphere, we may begin to feel hopeful. However, March can still be tough; littered with storms that still hold a high potential for snow. Despite the often miserable skies, the flowers are beginning to bloom and the lonely snowdrops are soon joined by many friends, from crocus to euphorbia, daffodil to winter cherry, and I am happy.

Though March often has a difficult start, by the end of the month, the clocks will spring forwards, and British Summer Time will begin (in theory!). For now, let's just enjoy the time for what it is, wild and full of hope. If you haven't already started to plan a holiday by now, what are you waiting for? We all need something to be excited about.

In this chapter, we will be testing your resolve, as well as sampling a couple of treats of the season and giving you a hint of what's to come in the warmer months.

Be out in a storm (or at least watch one)

In like a lion, out like a lamb

March, like many months, has its own proverb. You can easily grasp the idea behind it. At the beginning of the month it is still very much like winter, wild and windy, but as it draws to a close we head towards mid-spring and – hopefully – milder weather. There are many origins of March's proverb but the one I like the best is the story from the stars. As March arrives the rising sign is Leo, the lion; come April we move into Aries, not strictly a lamb, but 'out like a ram' just doesn't have the same ring to it.

It makes sense that March is so wild; as the Earth in the northern hemisphere heats up, it can make March a windy month. But any high winds this month will help to clear fallen leaves and twigs. Plants adapt to seasonal changes, and as March and the growing season progresses, this natural clearing out of old, dead wood makes way for new plants to bloom. This process is another lesson from nature we could apply to our own lives, so don't let the idea of getting a little wet make you housebound. You will dry, and when you do, you will feel drier and cosier than you ever did before. Let's make the most of the wildness this month brings.

Here's how

1 Think about where you want to see the storm from; woodlands in winds of above 40mph, which is when small twigs and branches break and fall, are not advised, for example, but I have survived worse. However please don't risk getting hypothermia, blown off a cliff or struck by lightning.

2 Get your clothing sorted. If you want to be out for a while then you will need full waterproofs, but if you are just dashing into the street for a couple of minutes then you could only need your shorts, giving the neighbours something to talk about. Do be aware though that you don't want to be far from dry clothes at this time of year.

3 Go outside for as long as you dare; feel the wind and rain on your face, smell the air and appreciate the sheer power of nature.

4 While you are practising today's activity, be aware that the air around a waterfall contains about 100,000 negative ions per cm^3. These are the good ions, the ones which remove techno-stress and ground our bodies; compare this to a measly 100 per cm^3 in the average office and you can see why you will feel invigorated after just a short time out in a storm.

5 When you come back in, after dealing with any wet clothing, make a good hot drink and enjoy the energising feelings you will have experienced, courtesy of the weather.

Make a spring flower bouquet

Studies have found that hospital patients take fewer painkillers after surgery if they have views of nature from their beds, that filling your home with flowers and plants can improve concentration while lowering stress levels, and that people living on streets lined with trees are significantly less likely to take mood-enhancing drugs like Prozac. After the colourless winter, so sparse of flowers and vegetation, I can't wait to get some spring flowers into my home, and judging by the supermarket shelves, neither can anyone else.

Don't settle for a bouquet from the shops though; not only is the flower industry an environmental disaster (producing mountains of single-use plastic, using masses of polluting agrochemicals, generating tonnes of carbon dioxide in transportation and using fossil fuels unwisely to artificially light, heat and cool the flowers), but also home-grown flowers are far more fulfilling to handle and bring you closer to the things that keep you well. Daffodils are the symbol of spring, flowering normally around the equinox in late March. If you haven't grown your own, there are lots of shops where you can find pretty cheap ones that are not heavily packaged and are likely to have come from the daffodil fields of Cornwall, Wales, Scotland or Lincolnshire, so less heavy on the transport miles too. With a small bunch of these, some foraged goods and an attractive container, you can make a beautiful display.

Here's how

1   Try collecting some little extras from your local area to go with your daffodils, like silver birch twigs – not yet in leaf but with beautiful buds – and greenery from conifers.

2   Putting your bouquet together is a really simple process; it can be made in your hand. Each stem you add, turn the bouquet slightly anticlockwise and add the next in a spiral. Try to balance out your blooms and greenery, varying the different textures.

3   When you are happy with the display, trim all of the ends to the same size and put in water while you prepare your container.

4   Choose an appropriate container; this can be a traditional vase if you choose but there are plenty of other options, like old milk bottles, test tubes or clean jam jars. Remember that displays generally look better when the flowers are twice as tall as the container.

5   To make the bouquet last longer, add a little homemade cut flower food: ½ tsp. vinegar, 1 tbsp. sugar and ½ tsp. household bleach in about a litre of water. Pour this mixture into your chosen container and gently place the bouquet inside it.

6   Removing wilted blooms or greenery and replacing with fresh ones will allow you to enjoy them as long as possible.

SUPPLIES

A bunch or two of daffodils

Floristry snips, secateurs or some good scissors

A selection of vases or other suitable vessels to choose from

Vinegar

Sugar

Household bleach

Plant a nectar bar

If you look closely, there are wild flowers everywhere, including in tiny urban green spaces, and there are still places in the British Isles where you can witness impressive displays of them, like the miniature ones that inhabit the slopes of the Yorkshire Dales. You don't have to wait until you can get out to these places. I like to see them at home, and in planting some, you will be doing your local wildlife a huge favour too. Since the Industrial Revolution there has been a rapid decline in habitats, alongside an increase in the use of pesticides in our gardens and farmlands. This has had a negative impact on our bees and other insect life, and if you value their contribution to our planet – which you should – then it's good to give something back.

We don't all have the space for a whole meadow – more's the pity – but you only need an old bucket full of wild flowers to create a lasting splash of colour throughout the summer months and provide a nectar bar for the bees and butterflies.

Here's how

1 Make sure you select your site to suit the wild flower mix you have. Be aware of the type of soil in the ground or container and any micro-climates (particularly hot, windy or frosty spots). The seed packet will indicate the flowers' ideal growing conditions; some prefer acidic soils, some like full sun, while others do well in the shade, but most wild flowers are pretty hardy.

2 Make sure your container has some holes in the bottom for drainage and put in some broken bits of pottery, or small stones, to help the water flow.

3 Mix up equal amounts of sand and compost and fill your container up to about an inch from the top.

4 Sprinkle some seeds from a wild flower mix, but go lightly to save yourself the job of thinning out later on. Cover with a little of the compost mix, water and wait. I'm afraid that's all you can do, it's going to take a while, but patience is a virtue – apparently – and by July you should have a pot bursting with flowers, which will last you and the bees through to the autumn.

SUPPLIES

Wild flower seeds

Container such as an old bucket, plant pot or old sink

Broken pottery or small stones

Sand

Compost

If you have no outdoor space at your house at all, you could try a little guerrilla gardening in your local area. Bee bombs are available online and in many shops, and consist of seeds rolled in wet mud that is then dried, but if you don't want to buy or make these, sprinkling seeds is enough.

Find an area of wasteland and lightly sow hardy wild flower seeds, like poppies, ox-eye daisies and foxgloves. These plants will sow seeds every autumn, and if they are happy in the spot you have chosen they will multiply dramatically.

Eat wild spring pesto

I do enjoy all times of year, but spring has to be my absolute favourite. Autumn is sleepy and full of colour, but it can be pretty drab, especially when the leaves are gone. Winter allows time for hibernation but it always goes on too long, and summer is fantastic but once it starts, you know it will come to an end and to be fair it's never as warm as I'd like it to be.

Spring, however, is full of hope. Maybe the summer will be long and warm, perhaps all of the courgettes I grow won't be eaten by slugs, possibly I will have time to get out and plant more flowers in the urban wild. At the beginning of spring, potential is unbounded, and nothing quite heralds its arrival more than the smell of wild garlic in the local woodlands.

Wild garlic has many names: ramsons, wood garlic, bear garlic and onion stinkers, to name a few. As humans, our bodies have been used to seasonal food way longer than they have known any processed food and it is good to give them a vitamin boost using plants from the local area. There are no air miles either, or wasteful packaging, so it's a win-win.

As with all foraging, firstly make sure you can properly identify what you are collecting. It is difficult to mistake wild garlic due to its pungent smell, but do be aware of Lords-and-ladies. It has similar glossy leaves – though spear shaped – and can be deadly poisonous. Even a tiny nibble will make your face go numb.

Remember when foraging to take only what you need – a small handful of leaves are enough for a little batch of pesto – and pick only the best quality.

You can use the normal basil to mix it with but I use parsley – a good blood cleanser, available all year round and easy to grow yourself – and sunflower seeds – much cheaper than the pine nuts that are traditional for the recipe but equally as tasty.

SUPPLIES

Small handful of foraged wild
 garlic leaves
Small handful of parsley
Small handful of sunflower seeds
Small handful of grated parmesan
Sunflower oil
Lemon juice

Here's how

1   Give your wild garlic leaves a good wash to
     remove any beasties, loose soil or dust.

2   To make the pesto, simply put the wild garlic,
     parsley, sunflower seeds and grated parmesan
     in a blender with a glug of sunflower oil and a
     splash of lemon juice, blend to the consistency
     you like and enjoy.

3   That's it, simple. Enjoy served with warm pasta,
     toast, in mash or soup, or however you fancy it.

Spring wild weather activity:
Homemade reed diffusers

We have already looked at how our sense of smell can improve our well-being. Scientists have now found that nature can benefit us even when we are not out in it, and let's face it, sometimes you just want to be indoors. Scientists in 2009 carried out research where participants stayed in a hotel room with certain essential oils, typically those found from a forest, being pumped through the air conditioning. Findings suggested that people had similar lowered stress responses and improved immunity to those achieved from being out in the woodland. So bring a little forest pharmacy home with you with these simple diffusers.

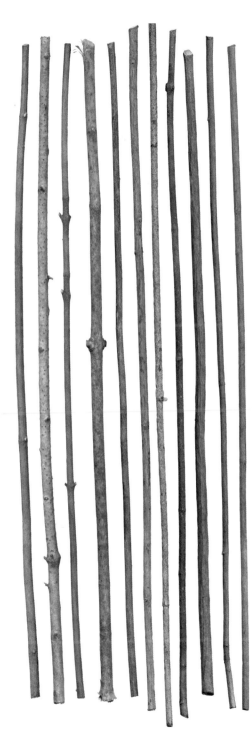

Here's how

1 Collect your materials, you will need:
   - A glass jar with a thin neck
   - 60ml carrier oil such as sweet almond oil or fractionated coconut oil
   - 2 tbsp. vodka
   - 15 drops of essential oils, for example try this happiness blend, it's one of my favourites: 5 drops orange, 4 drops frankincense, 3 drops juniper berry, 3 drops pourable benzoin

2 Go into the woods for a walk and collect 5–10 sticks, roughly 25cm long and 0.5cm in diameter. Hazel sticks are the best. If you don't want to do this you can just buy pre-made pieces of bamboo.

3 When you are home, use a potato peeler to remove the bark, being careful of your fingers.

4 In the glass jar, mix up the carrier oil, vodka and essential oils.

5 Soak the sticks in the fragrance for an hour or two.

6 When the ends are saturated, turn the sticks over and enjoy.

7 Turn the sticks every couple of weeks to keep the scent fresh.

April

At last, a month really worth waking up for! Sun streaming in through the windows in the morning and nights increasingly lighter. Yes, it can still be cold – average temperatures only a high of about 13°C and a low of 4°C – but we can get some really hot spikes in April and, due to the increase in daylight hours, the time away from work just seems to hold so much more potential. By the time you come indoors in the evening, you can feel like you have spent a really significant part of the day outside.

This month we will be welcoming the return of spring for real, taking advantage of the increased light, preparing for the summer and sampling some of the finest wild foods nature has to offer.

Plant something and watch it grow

In the 1980s in America a major experiment was carried out. Scientists built a self-sufficient dome in southern Arizona and opted to move in, with no resources going in, or out, for two years. Known as Biosphere 2, it was a completely closed system, much like our beautiful planet, and a massive achievement built on many years of scientific research from numerous countries. Needless to say, there were difficulties, but when they emerged two years later from the biosphere, the inhabitants of this mini world had largely got to grips with maintaining the system, and their own bodies were healthy too.

There were a couple of findings from this major research project that really inspired me and that hint towards how we can be part of the solution to the problems we are all too aware of in Earth's own biosphere:

- The scientists said the biggest engineering mistake made in the construction of the dome was leaving bare concrete. The concrete caused a chemical reaction that depleted the dome's oxygen content, something it took sixteen months to remedy.

- They found that any areas with sunlight but without a plant were a waste of space, given that plants were essential for both food and for dealing with carbon dioxide.

I use the latter finding as an excuse any time I want to get a new plant, or spend time down at my allotment. Contact your local council to find out if any are available near where you live (see link in Resources on p. 220).

March and April are the big planting calendar months but I tend to leave most things until April. With the increase in light and warmth, seeds planted at this time generally catch up with anything pushed into the cold, March soil, so it makes sense to wait. Come April, there isn't much you can't get into the ground, or into protected seed trays indoors.

First you'll need to decide on your own needs. People say the best way to success with plants is to only grow what you like and what likes you back. Leeks, for example, like me, so they are something I always grow. Onions, on the other hand, do not, so I've given up on them.

If you have the space for an outside pot or window box there are mountains of things you can try. How about a dwarf cherry tomato such as 'Tumbling Tom', courgettes such as 'Midnight', a nice mini variety, short carrots such as 'Paris market round', or aubergines, such as 'Long Purple'? If you prefer flowers, they are very rewarding too; dwarf multi-stemmed sunflowers, for example, will provide you with some cut flowers for the house. Dwarf nasturtiums brighten up any corner, an added bonus being that their leaves, seeds and flowers are all edible, with a delicious, peppery taste.

If the only growing space you have is inside, don't fret, there are plenty of things to choose from. With just a window ledge you can try:

- **Pea shoots** Buy a cheap box of dried marrowfat peas from the supermarket, rather than expensive ones from the garden centre. Soak them overnight and plant them in a couple of inches of compost in proper trays, or old plastic fruit containers. Harvest when they are 15cm tall.

- **Salad bar** You may not get full-sized lettuces but micro-greens are packed with vitamins and are normally quite expensive to buy. Growing your own is easy, cheap and there is a huge list to choose from including carrots, broccoli, amaranth, daikon radish, chard and much more. Remember you will be harvesting these as babies, so simply trim them with kitchen scissors and then get started on sowing your next crop.

- **Chillies** These guys like heat, so a south-facing windowsill is best, and don't water them too much, they will not thank you for it. They will only need a 15cm pot at full size, so are suitable for smaller spaces.

A variety of herbs can be grown to suit your available space too. Marjoram, sage, rosemary, thyme, chives, lemon balm and even bay trees all grow well in tubs outside. They are all perennial too, which means they will come back year after year and they tolerate quite a level of neglect. You can buy these as small plants, which should only set you back a couple of quid. Basil, coriander, parsley or mini window box dill can be grow from seed in pots on the kitchen windowsill. Growing fresh herbs gives you immediate access to their differen healing properties; thyme, for example, is antiviral. I add it to most dishes, including scrambled eggs, which is divine. Lemon balm, on the other hand, is calming; it makes a relaxing tea, or wine, which helps you sleep. Parsley is a blood cleanser and a good alternative to basil in pesto (see p. 60 for recipe).

(see p. 60 for recipe)

SUPPLIES
Seeds of your choice
Window box or other pots/containers
Compost

Here's how

1   Check the requirements of your seeds. All seeds are handled slightly differently and they come with instructions on the back of the packet. Generally though, you will only need compost and seed trays or pots.

2   As a rule of thumb, fill a seed tray or modular pot almost to the top with seed compost (this is really just compost with a little added sand for drainage, which you can always make yourself). Tap it down gently, sow your seeds on the surface and cover with a little more compost. Water lightly, label, and put in a warm place until you see the first leaves begin to appear, when they will need a little more light. When the first true leaves appear (they all have seed leaves which are followed by 'true' leaves), the plants may need to be thinned out, potted on, or moved to their permanent location.

3   Make a point to notice them growing; planting something and keeping it alive actually boosts your level of happiness.

4   Remember to enjoy your first harvest. I've been growing fruit and veg, in an urban environment since I was five and I am still excited to add home-grown food or flowers to the house, so make sure you appreciate your efforts.

Watch for the first swallows

Depending on where you live, as March ends and April begins, the first swallows start to arrive in the UK after spending the winter 10,000km to the south, as far away as the Sahara Desert. These tiny birds, only 18cm long and weighing around 20g, feed solely on insects and are way more fuel efficient than your family car. They pass through monstrous storms, high temperatures and a wide range of landscapes before they reach our native lands every spring.

In times gone by people believed that in autumn swallows left us to go to the moon, or that they overwintered in the mud at the bottom of ponds, but today, we know the truth. If one chooses to nest anywhere on your property, just pause for a moment to think about what they are capable of, how much they deserve a rest, and instead of finding it annoying, as some people do, think how privileged you are that they have chosen to nest and raise their young with you. Who knows how they decide it's time to make the journey northward, but when they do it's worth a little flutter with your family and friends to see when the first will appear in our landscape.

SUPPLIES
Identification guide, if you feel you need one

Here's how

1 Firstly, know what you are looking for. Look in a bird book or refer to the RSPB's online bird identifier guide (see Resources, p. 220).

2 Gather some friends or family in early April and place your bets. Set up a messaging group if you like and then start spotting. First one to spot a swallow wins a bonus prize. How you will verify this sighting depends on how much you trust your loved ones.

3 To be the first to see them, make sure you get the right time of day. The best time to see swallows is during the early evening, just as the sun is setting. Here the insects are at their best and the swallows can be seen – and heard – swooping and chattering during their evening feed.

4 Venture out of the house. Swallows can be found around towns and gardens, and are known for congregating on overhead wires, but they are likely to be more numerous around grassland, heaths, wetlands and farms. They especially like catching insects found around cows (or water buffalo during their winters in Africa), so find a place with outdoor livestock in your local area. If you don't know one then it gives you the time to explore.

Interestingly, the way a swallow flies can predict the weather too. If they are flying high, this means that because the air pressure is high so is their food, and good weather is upon us. Flying low, however, means that the air pressure is low and bad weather is likely to arrive, if it has not already.

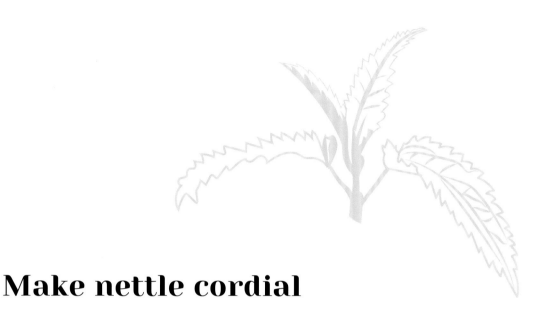

Make nettle cordial

Nettles are a really underused resource in this country; they are prolific and versatile, packed full of vitamin C and really delicious, much better than they sound, I promise! I have a book called *101 Uses for Stinging Nettles,* which explains the use of the plant from fibres to food, fabric dye to medicine, but my absolute favourite entry is number 101 – Erotic uses – which sends my students into fits of giggles every time.

Urtication is the name given to the practice of using stinging nettles to stimulate the skin for therapeutic reasons or for pleasure. It was popular in Victorian times when English mistresses used to beat their masters with nettles to – er – encourage them. Well, whatever takes your fancy I suppose!

Perhaps you would rather practice some of the other uses for nettles, and as a food they are fantastic, not just because of their vitamin and mineral content but also because of their herbal properties. They are an important spring tonic and a fast-working anti-inflammatory, among other things. When I first started cooking wild foods I made my parents a spring green pie, which included nettles. My mum had been having problems with her knee for weeks, to the point of finding it incredibly painful to get down the stairs. The morning after eating the pie the pain was gone – completely. On the next page is a recipe for a delicious nettle cordial that will keep for a year – the perfect pick-me-up any time you might need it.

Approximately 400g nettle tops
400ml water, preferably filtered
275g granulated sugar
Colander
Pan sieve
Glass screw-top bottles

Here's how

1 Wash nettle tops in a sink of cold water – make sure you are using gloves!

2 Place in colander and rinse with cold water, leave to drain slightly.

3 Meanwhile dissolve the sugar in a pan with the water.

4 Add nettle tops and bring to the boil. Simmer for 5 minutes.

5 Remove from the heat and allow to cool.

6 Strain the liquid through a fine sieve, squeezing out as much juice from the nettles as you can. Note that the sting has gone from the leaves now.

7 Bottle in sterilised containers. The cordial will keep for up to a year.

8 Serve as a drink made with still or carbonated water, use in homemade ice-cream or mix with icing sugar as a cake topping.

Foraged pakoras

Living in Bradford, the curry capital of the UK, I have been lucky enough to go on several cooking courses, the best by far being run by Kaushy Patel from Prashad, the award-winning Gujarati vegetarian restaurant in West Yorkshire. What a woman; full of love and passion for her food, which really shines through in the flavour of everything she makes. During one of the courses at the cookery school in Halifax, her husband joined us, adding herbalist knowledge to some of the ingredients we were using, making it an all-round fulfilling and inspiring day.

So this is the recipe for a Prashad-inspired, wild food pakora, designed and made with love and I tell you, if you like curry, you are seriously going to get on with this one. As always be careful when gathering wild food; make sure it is in an area away from pollutants or weed killer and ensure you can completely identify the things you are picking.

SUPPLIES

Pan, such as a chip pan or wok

Slotted spoon

Kitchen roll

Sunflower oil for frying

Filling ingredients

1 large potato

Good handful of ramsons (wild garlic), washed and finely chopped

Good (gloved) handful of nettle tops

I know we've used these ingredients already, but they really are so bountiful it would be a crime not to continue using them through the spring!

Masala ingredients

2 green chillies with seeds

2 cloves garlic

1cm root ginger, peeled

Batter ingredients

175g chickpea flour

1 tsp. plain yogurt (optional, but it makes the batter fluffier)

1 tsp. coarsely ground black pepper

1 tsp. salt

2 tbsp. granulated sugar

1 tbsp. ground coriander

1 tsp. medium chilli powder

½ tsp. turmeric

¼ tsp. bicarbonate of soda, not essential, but it makes the batter lighter

Here's how

1. Put the potato, whole and unpeeled in a pan of boiling water and cook until softened, about 30–40 minutes. Cooking the potato in this way stops it taking on too much water and losing the flavour. Afterwards drain, cool, peel and dice into ½cm cubes.

2. Wash the nettle tops in a sink of cold water, using a gloved hand. Place in a colander and rinse again with fresh water.

3. Put washed nettles in a pan with a splash of water and wilt as you would spinach. This takes the sting out of them. Put back into colander and allow to cool. Then squeeze out as much water as you can and chop finely.

4. Meanwhile make the masala by chopping the chilli, garlic and ginger finely, or blending in a food processor. Tip: use a teaspoon to peel the ginger, it's much quicker and wastes less flesh – thanks again Prashad.

5. Place all of the batter ingredients into a large bowl and mix together with your hand. Add the masala and 50ml of warm water, mixing thoroughly.

6. Add 50–75ml of cold water and bring the mixture to a firm batter.

7. Stir the nettles, ramsons and potatoes into the batter until all ingredients are combined.

8. Heat 15cm oil in a large pan, I use a small wok. Be really careful with this stage; stay focused on the hot oil throughout the process.

9. Add several teaspoons of the batter mixture to the pan and cook for about a minute, then turn them over and cook until golden brown.

10. Remove from the pan with a slotted spoon and drain on some kitchen roll.

11. Repeat the process until all the batter is used.

12. Serve warm with fresh mint raita.

May

Ah, May, my long-standing favourite month. Much better than the summer itself because it is so full of promise; all the potential warm weather is ahead of us, with long, light nights and higher energy levels to look forward to. May is actually known as a cold month but according to old proverbs, 'A cold May gives full barns and empty churchyards', so don't be too hard on it if it's not yet dishing out the goods.

That said, the flowers are starting to bloom, the trees are in blossom and generally life feels pretty sweet. If May were to be defined by one thing it would be the abundance of blooms.

This month we will be getting a little creative, interacting with the flowers and taking some much-needed time to relax.

Make daisy oil

Many of this month's blooms have useful herbal properties, and you can easily harvest some of these by soaking them in vegetable oil, a process known as maceration in herbalist terms.

The humble daisy is a common little flower, renowned for always bouncing back after it has been mown, or crushed by heavy feet. Most of you probably made daisy chains when you were younger, and in days of old some believed that a daisy chain bracelet would prevent the wearer from being stolen by the fairies. What many people have forgotten though, is the plant's Old English name, bruisewort, which highlights other things it has been used for. Making your own bruise ointment could not be simpler. The process takes a month but once you've made it, your daisy oil can be stored for up to two years. So find a patch of daisies, as always away from high dog traffic areas or roadsides, and collect enough to fill your glass jar (see supplies list) and lay them out on paper for half an hour or so to allow any insects to move out.

SUPPLIES
Your daisies
Olive oil
2 wide-necked glass jars
Muslin cloth
Sieve
Small glass bottles with caps or
  stoppers
Solid coconut oil

Here's how

1 Fill the wide necked glass jar almost to the top with the fresh blooms.

2 Cover with a good quality of olive oil (any vegetable oil will do, actually, but this tends to be the preferred type).

3 Leave on a sunny windowsill for about a month, shaking regularly to ensure the flowers are covered at all times to avoid them going mouldy.

4 Strain through a sieve into a clean, dry jar and then through a piece of muslin cloth to remove all the plant parts; these can be discarded into the compost bin if you have one.

5 Bottle, label and store in a cool, dark place. It will store for up to two years. This oil can be used externally on the skin.

6 To make a simple ointment, combine a little macerated oil with solid coconut oil, until it has the consistency of vapour rub.

7 Apply topically to bruises and sprains as needed.

Sleep in a hammock

The first time I ever stayed in a hammock overnight was during a weekend when around 15,000 lightning strikes were recorded in just four hours in the UK. We hadn't planned it that way, and to be honest it was a little scary at times, but it also made you feel incredibly alive. It's funny to look back on, and I remember my partner Henry muttering, 'I'm not sure what the protocol is here,' as the storm made its way closer through the trees. All I knew to do in a thunderstorm when camping was to get in the car, just as Dad used to tell us when we were little, but that wasn't an option on that night; the car was parked two miles away.

Anyway, I'm still here to tell the tale, and although I'm not recommending you go and get soaked through in a record-breaking storm, I am suggesting you spend some time in a hammock. I'm always surprised at how many people are really nervous about this but trust me, it is a beautiful, relaxing way to spend some time.

SUPPLIES

Hammock, or blanket if you really can't face a hammock (see step 1 on p. 90 for notes on hammock selection)

Roll mat or blanket for underneath your body

Here's how

1 Firstly you need to select your equipment. If you are planning to spend a lot of time in a hammock and hope to stay in one overnight, then look for one with a built-in insect mesh; this will set you back a few quid but they are – in my opinion – by far the best overnight option. If, on the other hand, you just want to hang out in one for an hour or so every now and then, go for something a bit cheaper; you can get them from the internet for about £10 and they come in all manner of beautiful colours. I tend to avoid the rope ones though, I don't find them nearly as comfortable.

2 Now make sure you have something you can put under your body; a camping roll mat is perfect if you have one, otherwise a blanket will do. This is essential; it's hard to relax for long when the cold air, even on a hot day, is licking at your back.

3 Next, find two suitable trees around four paces apart, though every hammock will differ. They don't need to be as big as you'd expect but look for ones that are a minimum of 15cm in diameter. Remember to look up too; you don't want to pitch under any dead branches, and look down; remove anything sharp or hard, just in case.

4 Tie one end of the hammock to your first tree. As a general rule, 'If you don't know knots, tie lots', but if you can, then use a figure-of-eight knot (top right photo), as they are easy to undo, even once they have held your weight for a while, followed by a couple of granny knots (bottom right photo) for extra security. You can also get things called tree huggers, which I use with a carabiner; they're really quick and simple to use.

5 Before leaping straight in, just gently test the hammock first, especially with new ropes as they do tend to stretch. (Once in the middle of the night I woke up in my hammock on the floor, as the ropes were new and had stretched overnight!) This also helps you check that the knots will not slip.

6 Now the only thing left to do is get in, relax and soak up the phytoncides.

If you do not have anywhere suitable for a hammock in your area, you have two options: take a bus to your nearest park, or take a blanket to a suitable piece of grass, and at the very least spend a little of your day lying down outdoors.

Make a natural gratitude journal

Research has found that taking time to be grateful for things in your life improves your mood, makes you more optimistic and helps you experience more positive emotions, while also reducing anxiety and depression and helping you to sleep. It also suggests that gratitude can lower your stress levels, reducing the stress hormone cortisol and improving your self-esteem and self-control.

A lesser-known fact is that nature actually boosts your creative potential, so putting these wonderful benefits together to spend some time outdoors in the sunshine, creating beautiful things, is the perfect combination. May is a month of abundance, making it a good time to hunt for natural materials to make a gratitude journal. If you don't see yourself as artistic then big pieces of plain paper can seem overwhelming; this is why I started producing tea bag art with my groups. These miniature works of art on tea bags come together beautifully in a journal and you can buy empty tea bags online for a few quid. For inspiration look at the work of Ruby Silvious, who makes absolutely stunning art on used tea bags.

SUPPLIES

Paper cut into small pieces or empty
  tea bags

Printing roller or brayer

Printing paint or basic poster paint

Scrap paper or old newspaper

Dried flowers

PVA glue

Here's how

1 Pack up a few basic bits of art kit so that you can make these small pieces of art outdoors and get the benefit of spending more time out of the house.

2 Find somewhere comfortable and take a moment to relax into the space. Mornings are very special and a good time this; every day is a new beginning and this activity is an opportunity to start each day with positivity. While you are creating your masterpieces, keep in mind all of the things you are grateful for in your life.

3 Try out some of the following techniques, aim to make at least three pieces to begin with:

- **Mono printing** Find something with a good texture, such as a leaf (bramble leaves are great). Use a printing roller, or brayer, to apply paint on one side, turn it over on to the paper (or tea bag) cover with scrap paper and apply pressure with a clean roller. When you remove the scrap paper and the textured object you will be left with its print.

- **Use text in artwork** Try creating some mixed-media effects by tearing out parts of an old worn book. I found a couple in charity shops; the best ones were a 1920s scouting handbook, which had some really quaint phrases, and some music scores, which look particularly fantastic.

- **Use dried plants and flowers** Press them between the pages of a book until they are dry and flat, then use them in your artwork by gluing them on using PVA.

4 While your artwork is drying, try this gratitude meditation:

> Bring your attention to your body. Be thankful for all it has done for you overnight, for all the systems that have kept you alive without you having to do anything at all. Your heart has continued to beat, your lungs have continued to breathe, all without you having to ask, or think about it at all.

> Close your eyes and observe your breathing, don't try to change it, just be aware of it and invite it into your body. Allow your mind to settle into your breath and if at any point it tries to wander, which is in its nature to do, just calmly bring your attention back to this.

> Take a deep breath in now and mentally ask yourself 'What am I grateful for?' Allow any thoughts, sensations, images and feelings to come. 'What am I grateful for?' Ask the question and let it go. 'What am I grateful for?' Repeat the question for a few minutes. Don't force an answer, just be open to your heart and whatever feelings come to you. Stay here as long as you need.

5 Relax into your body and slowly open your eyes, write down all of the things you can remember in your journal.

Honour your feet

When you walk on the beach, do you, like me, have the desire to take off your shoes and socks to feel the sand between your toes? Unless you are lucky enough to live by the ocean, you are probably spending most of your life with your feet squashed into some form of footwear. Learn to trust the instincts that call to you to go barefoot on the beach and give your feet the freedom to feel the Earth beneath them more often.

Grounding in this way has been found to strengthen your immunity, improve sleep patterns, reduce pain, relieve stress – including techno-stress and PMS – and increase energy levels. It's not important whether you walk fast or slow, travel ten metres or ten miles; it should be enjoyment not endurance, and all that matters is that your feet are in contact with the ground. With a little preparation you could honour your feet with a mini foot spa en-route.

SUPPLIES

Flask of warm water

Flannel and towel

Store-cupboard ingredients: a sprinkle of oats, salt or rose petals,

A couple of sprigs of mint or a couple of slices of lemon (optional)

Fine sea salt, a small handful

Vegetable oil or sweet almond oil, enough to just cover the salt

Essential oils, for example lemongrass and lime, 2 drops of lemongrass and 3 lime

Here's how

1 Before setting off on your walk, prepare a flask of warm water and grab a flannel to wash your feet down. You could even infuse the water with herbs, for added health benefits and to engage all your senses. Try adding one or two of these store-cupboard ingredients to the water:

- Oats (softener)
- Salt (detoxifier)
- Mint (freshener)
- Lemon slices (cleanser)
- Rose petals (emotional stabiliser)

2 Make a simple foot scrub in a small lidded tub: use fine sea salt, with just enough oil of your choice (I like sweet almond oil, it's a good all-rounder), and essential oils (lemongrass and lime are especially nice on the feet and boost your circulation too).

3 Find a place outdoors that you like to visit, it could be the woods, your local park or even your garden. Check the area for any litter or anything else unpleasant.

4 Remove your shoes and socks and notice the air around your feet; how do they feel to be allowed out?

5 Take a moment to become aware of your body in this space, from your feet to the top of your head, asking each bit of it to relax in turn.

6 Choose a one-metre square to investigate with your feet. Walk slowly and intentionally at first. Be aware of the heel of your leading foot making contact with the ground in front of you. As you transfer your pressure towards the toes of this foot, be aware of the release from the back foot as it leaves the ground. Place your feet carefully and with balance, feel the movement of the bones and the muscles within your feet.

7 Now change the pace and walk at whatever speed you wish. Maintain focus on the placement of your feet and also become aware of the surface underneath them. Try not to spend the whole time looking down if you can help it.

8 Finally, look for different textures to experience, perhaps a patch of soft moss, or some rough pebbles. Feel how much the grass seems like velvet after walking on a harder surface.

9 When you feel like you have done enough, find a nice place to sit and use the warm water to wash your feet down, saving some to wash off the scrub later.

10 Take some of the scrub in the palm of your hand and rub down all areas of your feet: heel, toes, arch of the foot, top, ankle. Be more rigorous in rough areas of the feet like the heel, and gentle on bony parts, or areas of thin skin.

11 Rinse your feet using the infused water again. Make sure you dry your feet properly and enjoy the sensation of having your feet truly pampered.

June

June is always a busy month for me, as more people want to get out into the woods in June than in January, but it's a good time of year to be busy. The nights are short and there is plenty of daylight to give us all energy. Make the most of it; you need to build up your stores for the winter ahead, which always comes round sooner than you would hope. It is more important than ever to find some time to just be, and I have started to block off chunks in my diary under the heading 'space', 'rest day' or 'my time', to do just that. I highly recommend you do the same; you cannot give from an empty cup, in fact forget the cup, if you are not giving from an overflowing teapot, you need some time for yourself.

If there is one plant redolent of the English countryside and gardens in June it's the rose, and there are plenty to be found all over the city too. This month we will be capturing some of the aromas in a sample of beverages and spending lazy days outdoors, practising more of the ever-important self-care.

Make rose petal gin

Well, we can't stay in beautiful June forever, but I can at least tell you how to capture a little of the month for drinking later. There are many options for flavouring gin, and I have tried a lot, but this is by far my favourite; it's quick, simple and incredibly tasty. You would think that it would be too floral, but that is actually not the case; you just get a beautiful waft of roses as you put it to your lips. This is best served in a gin balloon glass, which really does contain the aroma.

Try to collect your rose petals in the morning on a warm, sunny day when the volatile oils are strongest. All types of rose can be used, but try for one which has a good aroma; our wild *Rosa canina* is perfect and I prefer pink or red blooms to other colours, though as long as they have good fragrance they will work. Be careful to pick them from a safe spot, away from the potential of pesticides and away roadsides, where they will have picked up particulates from the car fumes, and remember the safe height rule: Always collect from above knee height. If you cannot get any fresh rose petals, this works equally well with the dried ones you can find on the internet. Always buy organic though, and remember that if you are using dried rather than fresh ingredients, you only need half the amount.

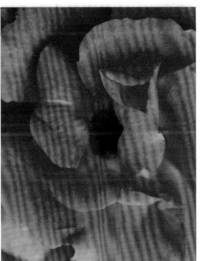

Here's how

1 Leave the rose petals on a clean tea towel to let the insects climb off but do not wash them, otherwise you will lose some of the flavour, as well as risking adding bacteria to your infusion from the water. Some people also cut off the white parts but I'm not that fussy.

2 The method is simple: put the rose petals in the jar, cover with the alcohol and leave for 24 hours. Taste it; if it smells of roses, it's ready, if not you can leave it for up to three days, checking daily. It is important that you do not leave it infusing any longer than the three days, however, as the petals can make the gin go bitter.

3 When you are happy with it, strain out the petals and put the gin in a sterilised glass bottle. Add sugar to taste, little by little.

4 Serve with a good-quality tonic and a cube of ice. Note: large ice cubes designed for the discerning whisky drinker, which due to their size don't melt too quickly, work equally well with G&T and are rather lovely too. Ice is important, not just to cool the beverage but also to improve its viscosity.

If you want to try other plant-based alcohols then remember this: as a general rule if the primary sense of an ingredient is smell, as it is with roses for example, extract through infusion. An infusion in cocktail terminology is basically submerging the plant material in a liquid (in this case alcohol) for a given amount of time. If the primary sense is taste, for example raspberries, make a syrup, which you can add to alcohol later. I explain this in a little more detail in September – see p. 156.

SUPPLIES

Lidded, wide-mouthed jar (the wide mouth is important as it is much harder to get the spent petals out of a bottle neck)

Rose petals to loosely fill the jar

Enough gin to cover, choose one with few botanicals already in it, as you want it to infuse it with the flavour of the roses

Caster sugar (roughly 25g per 750ml of gin)

Glass bottles

Find a sit spot

One way I like to spend a lazy summer day is to take a walk and find a place to which I am drawn, to sit or lie down. I rarely need to go far, even from my inner-city home. There is no aim, no plan, only a desire to simply be, to take in all the world has to offer in that moment. A warm breeze on sun-kissed skin, the hum of the insects going about their daily work, or the birds circling in the thermals overhead. It always amazes me how nature returns to a place when we are still. Just this moment a hoverfly has come to land on the end of my pen, causing a temporary pause while we investigate one another. The encounter is brief; they never hang around for long, he needs to make the most of these hot summer days while they are still here.

During one of these moments outside my tent in Pembrokeshire, I was sitting with Mia, my dog, and looking out over St Brides Bay. To my left there was a movement in the long grass, which soon revealed itself to be a ginormous dog otter. You never know what treats of the natural world you might notice when you choose for a moment to stop and be part of it.

SUPPLIES

A blanket

Some time for yourself

Here's how

1 Go to a nice place in your neighbourhood, even your garden or balcony. Choose a place with a tree, or flowers; if you really don't know anywhere like this in your environment you can take a cheap bunch of packaging-free flowers with you. Nature will find a way.

2 Take a mat or rug and sit down for a while. Pause for a moment to stop your mind from chattering about all the things you did not get done today, or need to do tomorrow. Remember this chattering is perfectly normal, it's in our mind's nature to do so, but right now, just for this moment, you are asking it to stop.

3 Be aware of your breath; feel the air entering your nostrils – fill your lungs and feel the rise of your belly.

4 Notice any points of contact your body has with the Earth, feel the support it gives you and know you can bring your attention back to these points if your mind starts to wander.

5 Watch for the effects of the elements. How does the wind influence the landscape? Where is the sun coming from and how does this impact on plant growth?

6 Who are you sharing this space with? Plant, animal, bird or insect?

7 Observe the sights and sounds in your immediate area, focus only on what is right here, right now.

8 Nothing to do, just stay here as long as you need.

Make elderflower champagne

The elder tree is a magnificent plant and I welcome its flowering every year, not least because it is the staple for our house white through the summer months. But it also makes a delicious cordial, which can be used as a long drink or as flavouring for ice cream. This little tree has much folklore attached to it, in fact it is said that you must never cut it down without first asking permission from the elder mother, the spirit of the elder trees, unless you want to bring bad luck to your house, and I for one abide by this rule.

That aside, it has multiple herbal benefits – the warding off of colds and flu being a particularly useful quality – and is a beautiful wild food of summer. This champagne is an excellent way of benefitting from its health properties, plus it is delicious, very low in alcohol and super easy to make.

When collecting the flower heads, choose bright ones with a sweet aroma. If they smell a bit sour then discard them. Give them a shake to remove the insects.

SUPPLIES

10–15 elder heads, depending on size
1kg sugar
2 litres water
2 unwaxed lemons, sliced
75g citric acid, or 1 tsp. cider vinegar
1 tsp. brewers wine yeast (optional)
Plastic bottles with screw-top lids

Here's how

1 Cut the main green stalks off the elder heads and keep the flowers. Put them in a heatproof bowl.

2 Make up the sugar syrup by simply dissolving the sugar in water on the hob.

3 When the sugar has dissolved, pour the syrup over the flowers, add the sliced lemon and citric acid or cider vinegar. These add vital acid, which stops the concoction going 'ropey'.

4 Leave at room temperature for 3–4 days, stirring every day to see if fermentation has started, evident in the bubbles. If after the first couple of days no bubbles appear, you can add a sprinkle of brewers wine yeast to kick-start the process.

5 After three days of successful fermentation, strain off the liquid, first through a sieve and then a muslin cloth. It is important to use the muslin as there will most certainly be tiny blackfly in it, don't worry, though, this is totally normal and has absolutely no ill effect.

6 Pour the champagne into plastic bottles and screw the lids on tightly. It's important to use plastic during this secondary fermentation as the carbon dioxide will build up, giving it that well-known fizz.

7 Store in a cool dark place for another couple of days, 'burping' the bottles daily to let excess air out.

8 Serve ice cold in a tall glass on a warm day.

Afternoon tea ceremony

I have always loved afternoon tea. One summer I travelled around Devon looking for the best on offer (the Women's Institute near Ilfracombe in case you are wondering). Funny thing really, considering that I don't even like tea.

Though tea is often viewed as a very British drink, it was actually exported from China to Japan and then from Japan to Europe around 2,000 years ago. To begin with, it was only the priests and upper classes who were allowed to participate in tea drinking, and it wasn't until the 1400s that common people could join in, and the tea ceremony was born. The Japanese tea ceremony, or 'way of tea', is highly ritualistic and choreographed down to the smallest hand movements, designed to deepen the friendship between host and guests. It is intended to bring your focus to the moment, and it is polite to talk about the ceremony itself for the duration.

It wasn't until the mid 1600s that Britain jumped on the tea train, which was down to a Portuguese princess, Catherine of Braganza, who was set to be married to King Charles II. When she arrived in Portsmouth, the first thing she asked for was tea. Portugal had long since been trading with Japan, and while it was new to the British, it was old hat for the bride-to-be. The British people were aware of tea for medicinal properties but it took royalty to convince them that it was a worthwhile pastime.

The notion of afternoon tea itself was not established as a British ritual until the 1800s, when the industrial revolution pushed dinner later into the evening and afternoon tea plugged the hungry gap in the late afternoon, for the wealthy at least. As with the Japanese tea ceremony, a range of fashionable accessories were developed to enhance the experience and in this 'fusion of British and Japanese rituals, you can enjoy the contrast between the mucky woodland floor and fine china, which I love almost as much as the thought of spending the morning up the allotment in the dirt and the afternoon being pampered in the spa.

Here's how

1 Traditionally British afternoon tea comprises three courses: sandwiches, scones and then cakes. Give yourself an easy ride and buy some sweet treats from the shop if you need to, this is meant to be fun, so don't create yourself extra work if you are not feeling it. The variety of shops is one of the perks of living in a city.

2 Make a selection of sandwiches with a variety of fillings.

3 Fill some scones with your favourite jam and clotted cream. There are plenty of scone recipes to choose from if you are in the mood to bake your own but remember, for a light texture don't handle the dough too much. Prepare your own wild strawberry jam (right) in advance if you have the time.

4 While green tea is the traditional drink in Japanese tea ceremonies, it makes sense to me to use what we have locally. Put a sprig of your chosen herb into a tea pot, individual cup or flask, pour over boiling water and allow it to infuse for a couple of minutes. Strain and serve with a little honey to taste. Alternatively, chill the tea for an iced drink. Try lemon balm for a relaxing brew, or peppermint for a refreshing hit.

5 Pack your tea, sandwiches and scones along with some fancy cakes and some plates and forks. I'm sure I'm preaching to the converted but please remember to take things home with you when you have finished. Other people's rubbish ruins any outdoor space.

6 All that is left to do now is to pack up your blanket, find a good book and head out somewhere beautiful for your luxurious afternoon tea in nature.

Ingredients
- 100g wild strawberries (if you don't have these then normal strawberries are fine)
- 2 tbsp. lemon juice
- 100g sugar

Method
- Remove the stems from the wild strawberries. Rinse, drain and add them to a small saucepan (if using normal strawberries then remove the white bit in the centre first). Add the lemon juice, this helps prevent the strawberries from scorching.

- Bring the strawberries to a simmer and continue to cook on a low heat.

- When they begin to release their juices (after about 5 mins), add the sugar and mix well until it dissolves.

- Boil rapidly to setting point (about 105°C).

- Cool slightly and pour the jam into sterilized jars.

SUPPLIES

A warm day

A blanket

A book

Some light refreshments (see left)

Herbs for tea-making, for example
  lemon balm or mint

Summer wild weather activity:
Make herbal gin bags

OK, so I do like the odd G&T, and what better way to spend one of your summer evenings than relaxing with a good cold beverage? You can improve a cheap gin no end with a few things you may find in your local wild.

Here's how

1   Collect or buy some of the following: elderflowers, lime flowers, juniper berries, dried apple, dried rose hips, dried orange peel, hibiscus flowers.

2   Ensure all of the ingredients are completely dry. For the flowers you can just lay them out on a piece of kitchen roll for a few days. The fruit however is better dried in a cooling oven or a dehydrator if you have one.

3   Mix the dried ingredients in a small bowl, carefully spoon into an empty tea bag, a fresh one of course, which can be bought online, add to a glass of G&T and enjoy!

July

It's funny; I spend a lot of time excited about what the summer has in store, and then when it gets here, it can be a little overwhelming. Nature is bursting at the seams, the growth is rapid, changing on a daily basis, and I can barely keep up with it all. Paths that were once impassable due to the sludge are now a challenge because of the undergrowth sprawling out over them. Make the most of it; they are often laden with wild fruits, which always taste better straight from the hedgerow than their poorer cousins found on supermarket shelves.

Believe it or not, the nights are already starting to draw in. The longest day in the northern hemisphere has passed, and the summer should have made itself thoroughly at home.

For me, July is a time to relax; not too much activity, no planting, growing or making, simply gentle connections with the nature in your urban landscape, and the ideas this month reflect just that.

Get to water

At the time of writing this we are in the middle of a heat wave, the best summer I can remember in a long time (if you like that kind of thing, which I do). Cities can be so uncomfortable in these conditions though, and all I want to do is get to water. Living a long way from the sea, I have to look for other options.

There are more than 2,000 miles of canal, 273 reservoirs, hundreds of rivers and around 400 lakes of over 5 hectares in the UK to choose from. All of these provide corridors or watering holes for resident and migrant animals. Today I had a very close encounter with the magnificent kingfisher down the canal; a brief flash of luminescent blue and it was gone.

In the unlikely event that you live nowhere near any of these major water sources, look at your local park. It's likely there are ponds or water features to cool by. Better still, you could create your own miniature haven for wildlife, and if digging a pond is out of the question, try making this simple plant-pot pond.

Here's how

1   Work out the size of pot that best fits your outdoor space; just a simple ceramic one from your local garden centre will do fine. If you have no outdoor space at all then choose a pot you would be happy to have in your house, like a brass bowl.

2   If your chosen pot has drainage holes, place a few rocks over them, then use tile caulk to fill in the gaps and make the bottom watertight.

3   Once the caulk is dry, fill the pot with water. Rainwater or filtered water is best, but if you can't access this then just fill the pot with tap water and leave it for a couple of days before adding your plants.

4   At the garden centre or online you can find a variety of deep-water or marginal plants for your mini pond. Think about the structure of the finished pond; as a minimum, choose one plant for height, one for spread and one to cascade over the sides.

5   Position your pond out of strong sunlight and close to somewhere you would like to sit, then enjoy the wildlife when it discovers its new home, which it surely will.

SUPPLIES

A container like a ceramic pot (see step 1)

Tiling caulk

Rocks for the base of the pond (see step 2)

Pond plants to fit container (see step 4)

Make mojito jellies

Mint has long been used as a beneficial herb; it has even been found in Egyptian tombs. It gets its name from Minthe, a Greek water nymph, who once tried to seduce the god of the underworld, Hades, and who paid for her promiscuity by being turned into the plant, forever to be trampled by the footsteps of others. The herb's mythology offers clues to its habitat. Mint likes to grow in damp, shady areas and is perhaps the most simple of all herbs to cultivate. You can easily start your own nursery by trimming the ends off shop-bought mint and placing the sprigs in water. Once they have rooted, pot into basic compost and water well. Mint will happily grow on a shady windowsill indoors, or in a damp environment outdoors. Be careful though, it spreads through underground rhizomes and can be a bit of a thug if left unchecked, so you may want to keep it in a container.

The minty fragrance comes from glands, mainly found in the leaves, where essential oils are produced. For the plant, this makes up part of its immune system; a way to deter predators, attract pollinators and to act as an antibiotic and an antifreeze. We use the essential oil in hundreds of products and know it as menthol. It is commonly used as a digestive aid, so what better combination than mint and rum?

You can make most cocktail recipes into a jelly shot, but the important thing to do is to keep the ratios the same, you don't want to overpower the flavours with alcohol, or get unsuspecting guests drunk after just one jelly. You can afford a little kick, though, and if you want to alter the flavour, change the rum and cold water proportions to suit your taste.

SUPPLIES

To fill 8 large shot glasses:

200ml rum

50ml cold water

10 sprigs of mint (see step 2)

400ml boiling water, to make the
  mint infusion

135g packet of lime jelly

285ml of boiling water, to dissolve
  the jelly in in

Here's how

1 Before you leave the house to forage, place the rum and cold water in a bowl and put to one side, or in the fridge if possible.

2 Head out to pick your mint. As usual this is best to do on a sunny day in the morning, when the volatile oils are at their best. Shake the stalks but do not wash them, then leave them aside to wilt for half an hour or so. If you don't grow mint or have any nearby, it's fine to use shop-bought.

3 Remove the leaves from the stem. Take a moment to breathe the fragrance in and then make a tisane with the mint by stirring it into the boiling water and simmering.

4 After about an hour, strain the mint and discard the leaves after squeezing them to get more of the flavour.

5 Reheat the mint-infused water in a pan until it's just boiling.

6 Combine the jelly with the boiling mint-infused water and stir until the jelly squares or crystals are fully dissolved.

7 Mix the jelly liquid with the chilled rum and water, then pour into shot glasses, silicone ice cube trays or into a small but deep baking tin. Set in the fridge, preferably overnight.

8 Serve chilled.

Savour a plant

We can find a deeper connection with nature by acknowledging how something came into existence, its life story, its history. Take for example a plant, in this case an edible plant like the juicy raspberry. It grows in a variety of habitats, from hedgerows to woodlands, and is found lining the field I am lying in now, just at the edge of the city. Inherent sun seekers, raspberry plants will spread by sending underground roots, finding new growing spaces where the nutrients are rich and the soil fertile enough for them to bear their fruits, like mid-summer jewels that glisten in the sun.

Many plants can be used to make delicious drinks, and we have already looked at a few. Remember though, if the primary sense is taste, rather than smell, then try making a syrup. You can use any fruit for this, but in July you can't go wrong with raspberries.

WILD RASPBERRY SYRUP

If you can't find any raspberries in the wild, then shop bought ones will do just fine, but do try to buy organic. Soft fruits are among the most heavily sprayed crops in UK farming.

Here's how

1   Rinse the raspberries in cold water and allow to drain.

2   Put them in a pan with the caster sugar and 400ml water, and bring to the boil.

3   Reduce the heat, add the citric acid and simmer for 15 minutes or until the raspberries are soft. Mash with a potato masher or with the back of a wooden spoon.

4   Allow the mixture to cool, then strain it through a sieve into sterilised bottles.

5   Store in a cool, dark place and use within three months.

6   Serve diluted with sparkling water, ideally outside, if you can find the right spot.

SUPPLIES

400g raspberries, freshly collected or frozen
300g caster sugar
¼ tsp. citric acid
Bottles with screw-top lids (old cider vinegar bottles are the perfect size)

Cloud watching

As I'm lying here to write this, I realise I really don't spend enough time lying down. As a child holidaying in the south-west, I spent a great deal of time looking up, whereas now it tends to be more of a conscious decision. Some evolutionary scientists worry about how this constant looking down, using hand-held technology, is going to affect our health; it's not how we have evolved to be. In the future, maybe we will all be slug-like creatures with nimble fingers, hunched over a computer keyboard, missing the necessary neck muscles to lift our head skywards and look up. I hope not. Let's you and I combat that grim future today and spend just a moment watching the clouds. In a busy schedule it can be hard to find the time for a full meditation but there are 1,440 minutes in a day, surely you have the time to spend one of them being mindful.

Here's how

1 Find a comfortable spot outdoors, in your garden, on your way to work through the city square, or in whatever environment you have available.

2 Give yourself a minute to notice the clouds overhead.

3 See how much the outer edges move like waves, hinting at their water content, as gravity rolls and morphs them through a constant state of change.

4 Notice gaps opening up to show the blue sky behind, and watch a small breakaway cloud until it vaporises and completely disappears, literally into thin air.

5 See the constant push and pull, like that within a teenage friendship group; look away for a moment and it has changed forever.

6 Be aware of your own mind and how it can't help but make patterns and find shapes in the cloud forms; it's just how we are wired, helping us to make sense of the world more quickly.

7 Marvel in how clever that is, and how lucky you are to be alive in such a beautiful world, where clouds that appear as light as candy floss, actually weigh an average of 500,000kg, the equivalent of 100 elephants, fantastic.

SUPPLIES
Just you

August

There's something beautiful about August, don't you think?
The summer days merge into one and the evenings are heady with the combination of heat, the scents of flowers on the air and the taste of that rose petal gin you made in June. The northern hemisphere has slipped into her summer clothes and is looking very comfortable in them, the haste of June and July has passed and you can really feel the unstoppable growth of early summer coming to an end. By the August bank holiday, there will have been at least a handful of days that remind you of autumn, and sure enough autumn will arrive, so eke as much as you can out of this month before we creep back towards the shorter days.

Despite making the most of the city, everyone needs a change of scene before the long winter, and this month we will be heading out of town, taking in the elements and spending whatever time we can, day and night, outdoors.

Go camping

Camping has been a part of my life since I was three months old; it's possible – due to my spring birthday – that I was even conceived in a tent. I've probably spent about five years of my life in one. Whether you have never been camping before, or are a hardened camper, this month it's time to get under canvas. Tent shopping is an enjoyable ritual but these days you don't even need to have your own. You can dust off the old tent in your friend's attic, or go to a glamping site where all the equipment is provided. If you want to buy your own, go and get some advice about what would suit your needs (I am of the opinion that with tents the N+1 rule definitely applies: one tent is never enough).

Please remember, no tents are actually 'disposable', and just because you may be able to buy one for peanuts these days, it does not give you permission to leave them littering our beautiful countryside. They are cheap because we don't always pay people a fair wage. Know that two nights in a natural environment can have health benefits that will last you a month, stimulating your immune system and increasing the quantity and activity of your natural killer cells, which are vital in your body's defence against viruses. It's probably as easy to go for one week as it is one night, so a good excuse to go for a bit longer and really build up those killer cells.

It's worth taking a bit of time over your packing and try to be mindful – a bit of a pilgrimage in itself. This prevents you from arriving at the site with no tent pegs, or with way more than you need.

135 Urban Wild **August**

Here's how

1 Find a campsite. Most are listed online but the more tranquil ones can be a little harder to find – I'm afraid I'm not giving any of these away! – so you will have to put a bit more effort into the research stage if that's what you're looking for. For me the campsite really does need to be by the beach.

2 If your tent is new, then have a practice at putting it up before you go; you don't want to be grappling with a new system in a summer downpour.

3 And that reminds me, check the weather. You can camp in most conditions but this is meant to be enjoyable, so don't push yourself too far if it is new to you.

4 Decide on how you will eat when you are there. Even if you plan to have all your meals in the local pub, you will still probably want to make yourself a brew, so some kind of cooker will be beneficial, or a flask of hot water I suppose. Obviously alongside this you will need appropriate cooking utensils and there's no harm in taking a couple from the kitchen.

5 While we are talking equipment, there are a couple of other things you should have: your own wash products, including a towel, some spare loo roll in a plastic bag, a torch and something you might use for entertainment, like a book or pack of playing cards – honestly, these do still exist.

6 Make sure you meet your own comfort requirements. You will need some kind of roll mat and sleeping cover, be that a king-size duvet or a travel-light sleeping bag, and personally I want a pillow these days, in fact two please. Don't let anyone make you feel ashamed about comfort; it's about being out, not being in a 'who's more tent-hardy' competition. Different trips will have different requirements.

7 Finally, after all of that, drive to the site, pitch your tent, turn off your phone, get some food and either head down the local pub for a cold beer or just chill at the campsite. That's it, relax. You will need to after all that packing!

SUPPLIES

This really depends on how you intend to camp!

Look at the stars

I know the stars are there all year, but I always associate
them with summer, and I can tell you much more
about the ones that are visible to us in the northern
hemisphere at this time of year. Without doubt this
is because I often live in my beautiful tent in August,
meaning I am outside all day and night. I love to watch
the darkness creep in and push the fading light to the
distant sunset. It's a magical time. On a clear night,
stars start to appear slowly at first (in fact some of the
brightest ones, which show themselves at dusk, are
planets) but as light fades and the twilight proceeds,
others are soon to appear.

I'm a bit of a snob with stargazing and do not approve of
the apps that mean you can just hold your phone up to
the sky to find out what you are looking at. OK, so they
have their place for orientation, I guess, but to me they
epitomise the instant-gratification society that we live
in. Besides, they don't give you the depth of knowledge
that helps you to remember them in the long term, or
the connection to constellations past. But look, if that
suits you, who am I to judge?

Here's how

1 To get a good view of the stars you really do need to get away from the streetlights, but it doesn't always have to be far. There is a playing field out the back of my house and we've even seen the Northern Lights there once. Of course, if you can get out of the city you will get a clearer view, and there are often organised walks you can join if you choose.

2 Always go from something you know, and then you can add more constellations to your repertoire. There are an estimated 70 sextillion observable stars in our universe (that's 22 noughts), and reading them is like looking at a map – it's easy to get lost if you don't have a definite point you recognise. Most people start with the Plough, also known as the Big Dipper, or Ursa Major – the Great Bear. It's simple to identify and has high-magnitude stars, which means it is bright and that it is in our skies all year round, not a seasonal visitor like Orion, for example.

3 Draw an imaginary line through the two stars on the Plough's 'pan'. Extend your line until it's five times as long, and you can identify the North Star, or Polaris, around which several constellations circle all year, including the sweeping dragon, Draco, clown-shaped Cepheus and the big W, called Cassiopeia. Being able to recognise Cassiopeia opens a whole new collection of stars, known as the Andromeda group, and my favourite of all the stories of our night sky.

Cassiopeia was the queen of Joppa and wife of King Cepheus. Together they had a daughter called Andromeda (look for the big smile in the sky just under the W). Cassiopeia claimed that she and Andromeda were the most beautiful creatures in all the land, more beautiful even than the sea nymphs. A mistake indeed, offending the nymphs and also Poseidon, god of the sea, who flooded the land, calling upon the monster Cetus to destroy the people. In a bid to save his kingdom, Cepheus, under instruction from the oracle, chained his daughter to the cliffs near their home. Just as the sea monster was about to take his prize, Perseus, entering from the west, on his way home from slaying Medusa, saw the princess, killed the monster and took Andromeda as his wife, as all good knights did back then. To pay for her vanity Cassiopeia was cast into the skies for all eternity, upside down.

4 By now you know quite a few of the major players in the map of the stars and being able to identify Perseus opens up one last gem, which I will share with you. As the Earth follows its orbit round the sun it passes through dusty areas of space from time to time. Some of these regions are repeated on a yearly cycle, and it just so happens that around 12 and 13 August every year the Earth passes through one of these dusty areas. This is one of the best times to see shooting stars; look to the constellation of Perseus for the best chance of spotting them, and remember how amazing it is to be alive on a tiny ball floating in space.

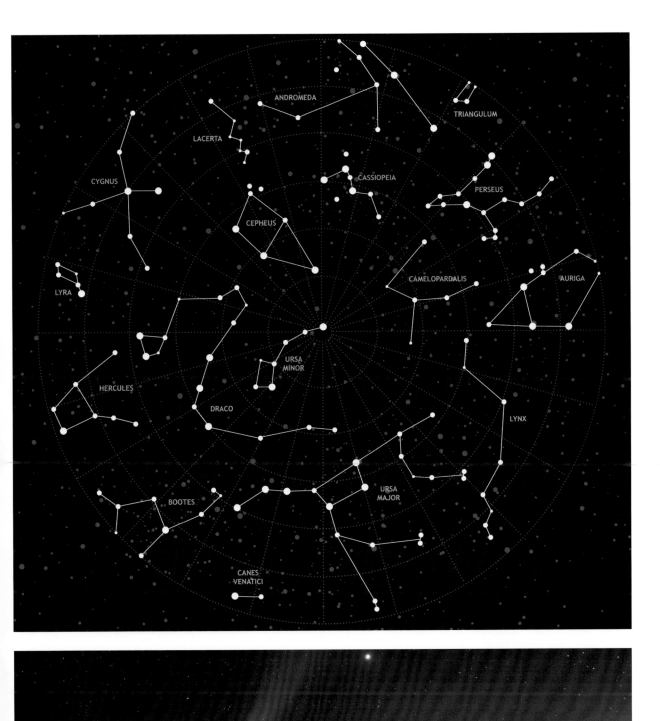

Sit by a fire

There is much debate over when humanity first began to interact with fire. As you probably know, it takes certain conditions to be able to create one, represented in the fire triangle with heat, fuel and oxygen. The first fire on the fossil record is from charcoal dated around 420 million years old; of course this was before our time.

Research shows that certain landscapes are only possible with fire; the African savannahs that our ancestors knew 7 million years ago would have turned to forest without them. You could assume that early hominids would have witnessed and taken advantage of the wild fires, most likely ignited through lightning strikes, with any attempt to control them merely opportunistic. Putting a date on the first controlled use of fire by early humans is pretty impossible – one-off hearths are extremely difficult to identify – but the most up-to-date archaeological findings show evidence of humans cooking on fires a million years ago.

Whenever the fascination began, fire is still a major draw for most. Some believe that fire heralds the start of our meditative practices, as early hunter-gatherers huddled round the hearth staring into the flames, though no one really knows for sure. So for this activity in August, sitting by a fire is something everyone should have the joy of experiencing.

SUPPLIES
Collected pine cones
Bucket of hot water
Variety of flame-colouring ingredients
(see recipes opposite)

Here's how

1 Make your fire. There are loads of instructions and videos on the internet on how to light a fire in a variety of different ways, depending on how much of a challenge you want, so I won't go into that here. I'll assume you can already do this and focus on a couple of other aspects of fire instead.

2 Practice mindfulness. Watching the flames dance and flicker against the night sky is mesmerising – we call it bush TV. Its natural ability to pull you in makes it the perfect accompaniment to meditation; it gives your brain something to focus on, which, if you recall (see p. 14), deactivates what is known as the 'default mode network', the parts of your brain responsible for rumination, planning and thinking about the past. Fire meditation requires very little effort; just stare into the flames, soften your gaze, breathe intentionally and if your mind begins to wander, just bring your thoughts back to the fire. You might want to consider the flow of energy between yourself and the fire, or imagine the fire burning away the old and making room for the new in your life, but you don't really have to do anything, just sit there, and for at least a part of the practice, sit in silence.

3 I also enjoy playing with colours in the fire, and coloured pine cones are superb, you can buy them online but they are not hard to make. Here are a few recipes, but please only use them if you are not also cooking on the fire, or wait until you have finished making any food.

To get coloured flames, try these additions, but wear gloves when you handle them as some of these might irritate your skin

- Red: strontium chloride (found in pet shops by the aquariums)
- Orange: calcium chloride (drying agent)
- Yellow: sodium chloride (table salt)
- Green: borax (cleaning product)
- Blue: copper chloride (often used in pyrotechnics)
- Purple: potassium chloride/potassium salts (sodium alternative salt)
- White: Epsom salts (often used as bath soak)

Colourful fire cones

1 Pine cones work better when open. If yours aren't open then you can bake them in a low oven for an hour or so and leave to cool.

2 Dissolve the colourant in a bucket of hot water, add the pine cones and leave them to soak for eight hours or overnight.

3 Remove the pine cones from the bucket and leave to dry, which can take a few days.

4 When they are ready just toss a few on the flames for an enhanced fire experience.

Swim in the sea

The ocean is my favourite of all environments. Lucky for me then that I live on an island, less so that I live in one of the most landlocked cities in the UK. It is always worth the effort to get to the coast, even if it is just for an overnight stay. But the best is when I get the chance to make the journey southwards for a couple of weeks; the mass exodus from my urban homestead to somewhere warmer (hopefully) and freer (certainly).A change of scene is vital to our survival, and for me is not complete without a trip to the coast. This book is about the urban wild, but we all need a break from time to time, and mindful swimming in the sea is a joy I can seriously recommend.

Here's how

1   Please be careful where you choose to swim; make sure it is somewhere that has no strong currents (see p. 220 for a link to the RNLI's safe swimming advice) and get in slowly so that your body can adjust to the temperature.

2   Stop once you have gotten over the initial shock of the temperature (I do swim in warm places but trust me, the North Sea – or Yorkshire Sea as we call it – is like daggers to the limbs!).

3   Now take some slow strokes. Watch the water as it is pushed away by the movement of your arms; see how much of it is influenced by you, no matter how gently you travel. Try to reduce your impact, making the strokes even more calm and even more steady.

4   Feel the water as it flows past your skin, knowing that all the hairs on your body are streamlined and are there to aid, not restrict you, in your movement through the water. Notice the air cooling your sea-soaked face.

5   Listen to the sound of the water as you glide through it, as it laps around your neck. What other noises can you hear? Maybe gulls in the distance, or the faint sound of the rope on the mainsail of a nearby boat.

6   Carefully take a few deep breaths in through your nose or mouth, feel the air cold as it passes into your nostrils and notice the change of temperature as it leaves, having been warmed by your body. When you inhale do you notice any faint aromas? Maybe the smell of seaweed from the shore or the salt in water?

7   Taste the salty water on your lips.

8   This experience can continue to feed your well-being long after the event, so while in this state of calm and in full appreciation of the present moment, try this pressure point programming:

> Using the finger and thumb of one hand, gently squeeze the area on the other known as the 'hand valley', the area of skin between the thumb and index finger. Engage your senses as you did above, soak them all in for just a couple of minutes, notice how calm you feel, how in control, how happy you are. Take all these feelings in.

> When you are back in your everyday life, all you need to do to bring back this moment and these relaxed feelings is to put gentle pressure on your hand valley. Try it when you are feeling stressed, or when you want to remember a time when you felt truly at peace. Trust me, this feeling can last for years.

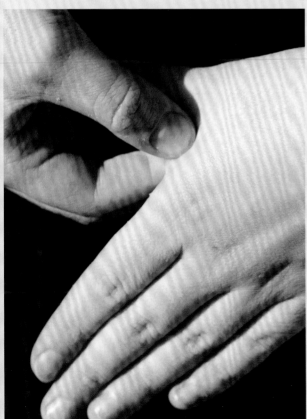

SUPPLIES

Swimming costume (in most places)

Towel

September

September is a beautiful month, such a shame it is tainted for many by the back-to-school vibe that signals the end of the freedom that the summer holidays brought. Let's not get bogged down by that feeling. It is OK to acknowledge a sense of loss as the summer slips into autumn. Still, the quicker we accept the transition, the more we can enjoy the nature on our doorsteps in what can often be a really bright and warm month. Let's not also forget the beauty this month brings as trees start to display the bounties of all their hard work and draw energy back into their winter stores resulting in a feast of colours not unlike a firework display.

September has a certain softness that only autumn can deliver, as the shadows lengthen and the sun moves southwards in our sky, taking its light and warmth with it. This month, of course, has to include an element of harvest, and we will be looking at food, drink and remedies from nature, as well as slowing down to match the energy of this time of year.

Wild herbal balms

There are many ways to extract herbal properties from plants for our benefit, and people working in different disciplines use terms in different ways, some of which we have come across already [X-ref]. You can easily capture some of the autumnal herbal harvest through a variety of methods, but to make a natural and beautiful balm first make a macerated herbal oil, which can be used in the recipe below. As a rule of thumb use half the quantity of dried herbs to fresh herbs. If you can't find them locally you can easily get them online, as always choose the best quality you can afford, organic where possible. Try herbs like:

- Eucalyptus (leaves), available throughout the growing season, used as a decongestant.
- Comfrey, known as knitbone (leaves and root), to heal damaged bones, sprains and bruises, and to remove splinters.
- Yarrow, sometimes known as woundwort (flowers, leaves and seeds), for nosebleeds, cuts and wounds.

A maceration is a quantity of herbs, chopped or ground and submerged completely in oil, which is left for a minimum of 10 days, though usually 3–4 weeks, then strained through a muslin cloth. When bottled and stored it will last for six months to a year.

SUPPLIES

5ml of your macerated herbal oil

15g beeswax

80ml sunflower oil

Bain-marie (for this I use a metal dog bowl over a pan of water, a heatproof glass bowl would work equally well, but don't use one you want to use for food again)

Kitchen roll for wiping excess wax from bowl (they don't wash well)

Small lidded jars

2–3ml essential oil (optional). Try a combination of eucalyptus and peppermint.

Here's how

1 Make the macerated oil as described above, and found in more detail in the daisy oil recipe from May – see page p. 86.

2 To turn your oil into a balm, put the beeswax and sunflower oil in a bain-marie, simmer until the wax has melted, add the macerated herbal oil and remove from the heat.

3 Add the essential oils while the fats are still liquid, quickly stir and bottle in a wide-necked jar immediately. Store for up to two years.

Bountiful berries and the art of eating mindfully

Blackberrying in autumn is perhaps the most well-maintained foraging ritual in the UK. At this time of year the blackberries are out in abundance, but be sure to pick before Michaelmas Day (29 September), after that it is said the devil has peed on them. An old wives' tale perhaps, but pretty sensible, as it tends to be around this time that the flesh can begin to harbour potentially toxic moulds. For the best quality fruit, check the part where the fruit was attached to the stem: if it is brown then discard, if it is whitish green it's a keeper.

Once you have found a good patch, pick no more than you need (including a few for the freezer to use later in the year), as there are many other animals that benefit from the vitamin boost before the long winter ahead. Now enjoy a few with a spot of mindful eating.

Here's how

1 Take one of the blackberries. Imagine you have never seen one before, and explore it with your senses. Turn it around in your hand. Notice the different colours around the surface, see how it reflects the light on each part of the cluster and how it is darker in the tiny crevices.

2 Take the blackberry to your ear, lightly roll it around between your thumb and forefinger. Listen to the juice inside as you squeeze it gently.

3 Now to your nose. Take a deep breath in and notice the smell. Rub it across the top of your lip, feeling its texture.

4 If you start to wonder what on Earth you are doing, just acknowledge those thoughts and carry on with the exercise.

5 Begin to slowly take the berry to your mouth, noticing how the arm knows exactly where to go. Place it in your mouth but don't chew, instead roll the fruit around for a little while, getting a sense of it on your tongue, at the front and at the side. Notice how your mouth begins to water in anticipation. Now slowly begin to chew, feel the juices exploding from the fruit, take your time with every bite. When you feel ready, swallow, sensing it moving down to your throat and into your stomach.

6 After a pause, take a second blackberry, this time spending a moment in appreciation of how this fruit has come into being. How a bud formed back in spring, containing a tiny pinkish-white flower. Consider that without a pollinator, like a bee or hoverfly, this flower would never have been able to transform into such a delicious treat. Be aware of how with sun, rain and nutrients from the soil, this tiny fruit swelled into the delicious, blackish cluster of berries you see before you.

7 Take a moment to congratulate yourself for knowing where to find this little gem and for taking this time to experience mindful eating. Now eat it slowly as you did before.

Wild mocktails

When I was 19, I worked in a cocktail bar in Dublin. There I learnt that a good mocktail perfectly combines a mixture of sweet, bitter and acid flavours. It's possible to make some great additions to the cocktail (or mocktail) cabinet with plants you find in nature.

Cordials and syrups are used to add both colour and sweetness – the nettle cordial from April and the raspberry syrup from July would both work well – and for the bitter element you can buy Angostura, or orange bitter, but it's also possible to make your own by infusing gin with beech leaves or brandy with cherries. These bitter elements are alcoholic, but are used in such small amounts they are considered a non-alcoholic mixer. For the final balancing act, you will also need a little tang of acid. These are often measured as 'a dash' (one-eighth of a teaspoon if you're fussy about that kind of thing) and can be achieved with citrus fruits, balsamic vinegar, cider vinegar and even red wine.

This month we will make the most of nature's harvest with this crab apple shrub. In a cocktail sense, a shrub is an acidic syrup usually made with vinegar or citric acid; the word comes from the Arabic word 'sharab' meaning 'to drink'. All varieties of crab apple are edible and can be found in ornamental gardens in the city, or on the edge of woodlands. The flavours will vary from tree to tree but all of them will have a sharp bite. First you need to find and collect them; choose a sunny morning if you can. Making the juice for the shrub will take up to a week, after which you will be ready to start mixing.

To get you started, you could try swirling a couple of drops of Angostura bitter around a tumbler, followed by a splash of elderflower cordial, a splash of crab apple shrub and topped up with sparkling spring water, but don't be afraid to experiment too.

Here's how

Ingredients

350g crab apples (tart cooking apples will do if you can't find any of these)

½ litre cider vinegar

450g caster sugar

Method

1 Quarter the apples; there's no need to core them. Put them in a pan with the other ingredients and bring to the boil.

2 Remove from heat, cool to room temperature, cover and chill for at least 24 hours and up to one week.

3 Strain the liquid off, discard the solids, then bottle and store for up to a month, or use immediately in your alcohol-free experiments.

SUPPLIES

Cordials or syrups made previously

Bitters

Acids

Mixers such as fresh orange juice, or sparkling ginger beer

Crab apple shrub (see recipe above)

Fancy glasses

Wooden cocktail sticks

Fruit pieces for presentation, such as melons, apples, berries or sliced citrus fruit

Optional garnishes of your choice for the glass rim (see right)

Try out different combinations for your concoction that allow for a splash of sweet and acidic, with the main ingredient coming from your mixers.

Finally, no mocktail is complete without the proper presentation, so here are a few suggestions to help you finish off your creation:

Ball – use a melon baller for small spheres of fruit, try apples

Drop – anything that sinks to the bottom, like a berry

Float – anything that floats, such as a flower head

Jewel – on a cocktail stick, try autumn berries

Rim – before filling the glass, run a quartered lemon around the rim, and then dip it in salt, sugar, desiccated coconut or grated chocolate

A slice or wedge – any fruit dropped in or balanced on the rim

Wheel – a full round slice with a notch cut out to wedge onto the rim

Flag – a wheel with a berry wedged in the middle and held with cocktail stick

Skewer – fruit pushed on a cocktail stick and dropped in drink

Spear – fruit on cocktail stick and balanced on the rim

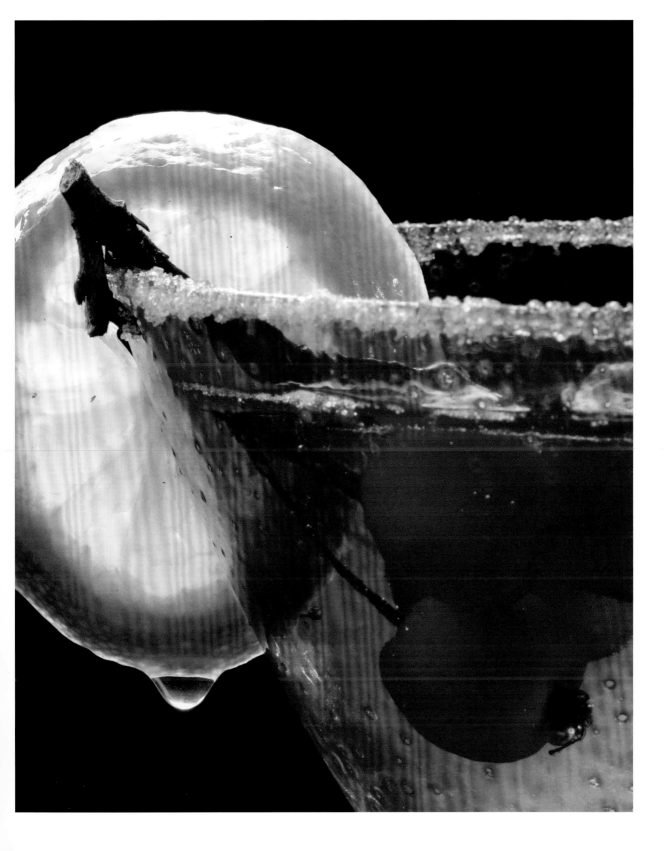

Rose hip vinegar

Rose hips are without doubt a superfood. They are packed with vitamins and minerals, in fact, 100g of rose hips contains twenty times more vitamin C than the same weight of oranges, plus they are easy to find at this time of year, so there are no air miles either.

Just after the war, my mother-in-law, like many children of the day, was paid to go out and collect rose hips so that they could be turned into a sweet syrup to keep the nation healthy over the winter months. They are a fantastic way to ward off colds and flu. My generation remember them for the itchy seeds we would extract from the pulp and stuff down the crisp, white school shirts of our unsuspecting friends to make them scratch like crazy. No longer a teenager, today I am more civil and absolutely love this rose hip vinegar, made into an immunity-boosting salad dressing for the winter.

Try to collect the hips on a warm morning. The vinegar itself will need to sit for about a month before use in the salad dressing, so September is the perfect time to make it for use in winter. It will store for a year on its own but for less time when you turn it into a dressing, so make the dressing up in small batches.

SUPPLIES

Wide-necked glass jar (I use a 1-litre jar)
Enough rose hips to fill the container
Enough cider vinegar to cover them
Toasted almond oil, roughly the same quantity as the cider vinegar
Whole grain mustard and honey to taste

Here's how

1   Wash the rose hips, prick each with a cocktail stick, or squash slightly (optional) and put in your jar.

2   Cover with the vinegar and leave in a warm place indoors for around a month, before straining through a sieve and bottling.

3   To make the dressing, combine your vinegar with an equal quantity of toasted almond oil.

4   Season with salt and pepper, then add the mustard and honey to your own taste.

5   Drizzle the dressing over salad leaves, or over finely chopped tomatoes, cucumber, black olives and a tin of chick peas.

Autumn wild weather activity:
Make a plaster print

There has been a crafting revolution over the last decade. Before the Industrial Revolution, our villages and hamlets would have been full of craftsmen and women such as weavers, potters, jewellers and rug makers, to name just a few.

People are beginning to realise how valuable and enjoyable these activities can be and how important it is for us to maintain knowledge of these crafts for future generations. Many require expensive equipment these days, but plaster is a cheap and accessible medium that even toddlers can master with little effort, and it is fantastic for picking up the detail of different natural materials.

Here's how

1   Collect some natural bits and pieces like seed heads, grasses and lichen.

2   Cut a cardboard tube down to 5cm segments.

3   Roll out some clay – any kind will do, even river clay – using a rolling pin. To get it flat have two 1cm thick wooden batons on either side.

4   Use one of the tube segments to cut out a round of clay.

5   Carefully push your found objects into the clay, gently roll over them with a rolling pin, then and remove each piece, leaving the indentation.

6   Put the tube segment back around the clay disc.

7   Seal the tube to a wooden board with clay sausages.

8   Mix up your plaster; as a rule of thumb start with the correct amount of water and add the plaster until it forms a little island, then mix together to a creamy consistency.

9   Pour the plaster on top of the clay disc and allow to set. For the first five minutes or so, gently agitate the board to remove the air bubbles from the plaster.

10 It is normal for the plaster to go warm, as it is cooling and also hardening.

11 When it is fully set, cut the tube open and remove all the clay from the plaster.

12 Left behind will be the imprint of your beautiful, natural finds.

October

As the harvest continues, October is a month to enjoy the fruits of our labours on the city allotment, and there is still plenty of wild food to be had, too. It's a good time to start planning improvements for next year's growing season, some of which you can plant right now. By the end of the month, autumn will most definitely be coming to a close. Like other creatures, we need time to transition into winter, with which comes a little preparation for the dark months ahead.

When we get a good October, the light is frequently more beautiful than in any other month, and it's certainly most welcome. If we are lucky, St. Luke's Little Summer will give us the typically warm period mid-month before the storms of Halloween appear.

This month we will be observing the change of season in our urban environments, preserving wild food to enjoy over winter and getting into the spirit of Halloween, whatever age we are.

Wild berry jelly

A vital part of autumn is making use of some of the vitamin-boosting berries that are widely available in this season. It doesn't matter what combination of edible berries you use as long as you stick to the basic ratio, and jellies are much easier to prepare than jam (because you sieve all the solids out later), set far more easily in my opinion and can be used in exactly the same ways. Bonus.

SUPPLIES

About 1.5kg mixed berries; try
  hawthorn for its heart tonic, elder
  for its flu-fighting properties
  rose hips for the vitamin C, and
  blackberries, if you have frozen any
  in September

750g granulated sugar

Juice of 2 lemons

Large pan

Jelly bag or muslin

Sterilised, lidded jars

Ladle

Jam funnel and thermometer
  (optional)

Here's how

1   Put all the fruit and lemon juice in a large pan, add
    water to just below the fruit line, bring to a low boil
    and then cover and simmer for an hour.

2   Mash the fruit in the pan and pour the liquid
    through a jelly bag into a glass bowl, leaving to drain
    overnight. Do not squeeze the bag as this will both
    burn you and make your jelly cloudy!

3   In the morning measure the amount of liquid you
    have, return it to a clean pan and add 285g sugar per
    600ml of juice. Heat carefully until the sugar has
    dissolved, then boil rapidly until it reaches setting
    point on your jam thermometer (105°C).

If you don't have a jam thermometer you can test for
the setting point by putting a little of the jelly on a
cold plate, letting it cool for a minute and running
your finger through it. If the mixture closes in over the
clean line you have made then it is not ready, if the two
parts stay separate it is done. This always takes me
longer than the 15 minutes the books tell you.

4   Remove the pan from the heat and scoop off any
    scum that may be on the top, then pour into clean,
    sterilised jars. I sterilise my washed jars by putting
    them on a low heat in the oven until they are too hot
    to touch without oven gloves.

5   Leave to cool and label with the name and date.
    Store in a dark place for up to a year.

6   Serve on warm toast, in yogurt, or in any other way
    you would use jam.

Make a bulb lasagne

You really don't need a lot of space to bring a bit of nature to your home, and October is the perfect time to plant up bulbs for the spring. Much of the work on the allotment has slowed down, and it's useful to reflect on your year, and to consider the actual and metaphorical seeds you would like to sow for the spring. It always amazes me that each tiny bulb holds all that the plant needs to become a new flower, and that a daffodil bulb can only be a daffodil, a crocus just a crocus, no other options or possibilities. There don't need to be any other options; they are perfect as they are, as themselves, just as you are, the only person on Earth who does you as well as you can.

Here's how

1 Make sure there are drainage holes in the bottom
of your pot. It can be a traditional plant pot, or any
other container, for example a large empty olive tin.

2 Fill the bottom of the pot with about 5cm of your
chosen compost.

3 Start the first layer or bulbs, choosing ones that
are bigger for the bottom, or ones that flower later,
they can be geometric or random for this style
of planting. Don't worry about giving them the
distance or depth that they say on the packet; they
don't need it if they are in a pot.

4 Add another 5cm of the compost mix, then
your next layer of bulbs, the smaller or earlier-
flowering ones.

5 Repeat the process until you reach the top of the pot.

6 Finally add the bedding plants and fill around them
with your compost. Bulbs do not give you an instant
display, so it's better to have some things which have
interest now. At this time of year there are more to
choose from than you think. I like winter-flowering
pansy or viola.

7 Just as in your own life, times where things look
dormant, as your bulbs do right now, are never really
so. There is always something going on under the
surface; we cannot and should not always be in a
state of visible growth. Water your plants lightly and
quietly await the promise of spring. While you are at
it, give yourself a break too. It's normal to need some
quieter times as the dark nights draw in.

Autumn light photography

The light is enchanting at this time of year. The shadows are long and all the land glistens. There are a couple of times each day that photographers consider the best for taking photographs, especially for landscapes. The first is golden hour. This is the period of time at either end of the day that is roughly an hour before sunset, or an hour before sunrise. During this time the sun is low in the sky and the rays are less bright than during the middle of the day, as they have to travel through more of the atmosphere to reach the Earth's surface. Because of the angle, it is also a time when shadows are longer, though less deep, which makes for interesting contrast. Another magical time for photography is known as blue hour. This is around twilight and is either just after the sun has set or just before it rises but when there is still an element of daylight. At this time the blue rays are the most prominent in the sky, giving a soft hue to photographs. Experiment with different times of day and see which ones give you the effects you like the best.

When you are feeling a little out of sorts, heading off to your nearest wild space to take photographs can be a great way to shake off the funk; it makes you stop and look, giving your brain something else to do. One little gadget I have enjoyed this autumn is a photo ball. They are about twenty quid from the internet and are really easy to use. You don't need to rush off and buy a fancy camera – most of us have a decent lens on our phones these days – and the purpose is to get outside, to relax and observe, not to produce award-winning photography.

Here's how

1 When there is at least a half-decent forecast, allocate yourself some time to go and play and head off to your local bit of urban wilderness, trying out different times in the day.

2 Tune into your area. Look for the best light in the scene, remember the way the ball works is by refracting light; when light hits the surface it bends and interesting things happen.

3 Once you have selected your subject, find a natural resting place for the ball. It can be propped up with sticks or placed in a bottle top to keep it still.

4 Generally, elevate the ball – if it is on the ground it won't capture the entire scene. There are exceptions to this rule, however; you could consider putting the ball in a puddle, or in a bed of leaves.

5 To really take notice of the landscape you are in, experiment with some long shots, which celebrate the whole environment, and some macro ones too, which pick up on tiny details.

6 Take a few different shots, and when you have one that you like, try turning the image upside down, putting everything in the photo ball the right way up again.

7 Use your images to make homemade cards, for times when you need to let people know you are thinking of them.

SUPPLIES
Camera
Photo ball

Carve a pumpkin

Pumpkin lanterns are not just for kids. You only have to look at some of the designs on the internet to see that they have come a long way since the traditional, triangle-eyed creatures that have adorned many a doorstep, lighting the way for expectant trick-or-treaters. Ideally it's an activity to be done outside, around a fire, but sometimes the weather is too miserable and you just don't want to go out; that's when to bring nature into your home.

Forget the plastic carving tools you can buy in supermarkets, they are completely useless and just more pointless single-use plastic, which will find its way to landfill, or our beautiful oceans. I have experimented with a variety of tools but the best by far are ones which have been designed for woodwork. I have a small box of woodcarving tools which cost about ten quid, plus a crook knife, designed for spoon carving, which makes short work of scooping out the insides. If you don't want to commit to that, then basic kitchen equipment will do the job.

SUPPLIES
Pumpkin
Permanent marker pen
Serrated kitchen knife
Spoon
Wood-carving tools (optional)
Gardening glove (for safety)

Here's how

1 Using a permanent marker, draw where you will be cutting out the lid. This can be at the top, as is traditional, or on the side, leaving the stem as the 'nose'. Cut a flat base, if needed. Be sure to cut a tooth-like point on either side, which will keep your lid in place when you have finished.

2 Draw the design for the rest of the pumpkin.

3 Use a bread knife, or other serrated knife, to cut the lid off and put to one side.

4 Scoop out the seeds using a spoon and lay them out on a baking tray to dry (see p. 182 for a quick and easy toasted pumpkin seeds recipe).

5 If you have a crook knife, use it to scoop out the flesh. They are sharp, so make sure you have a gardening glove on the non-tool hand and that your hand is not in line with the cutting action. If you haven't got one of these a kitchen spoon will work fine, it'll just take a bit longer. You could sharpen the edge with a grinder if you have one but it isn't necessary. Discard the stringy bits but leave the best of the flesh in the fridge for later (see p. 182 for how to make it into a lovely soup).

6 Now, using a small serrated knife, cut out the pumpkin design. Make sure that you are supporting the sides to stop the walls collapsing. If you are cutting from the outside, then apply a little pressure with your other hand from the inside, though make sure your hand is not where the knife will come through.

7 Once you have removed the main features you can add extra decoration by using a woodwork tool to engrave patterns, which do not go all the way through but let a little light shine out. You can also add extra holes with an apple corer, or hole cutters designed for working with clay.

8 Place a tea light inside, put the lid back on and position the carved pumpkin outside. If you have no outdoor space you can put it on your windowsill, with an LED light inside to minimise risk of fire.

THE BEST PUMPKIN SOUP

Don't waste the pumpkin flesh, it's not the most suitable for pumpkin pie but it makes a lovely soup.

Ingredients

- Knob of butter for frying
- 1-2 tsp. cumin seeds, depending on whether you had a small or large pumpkin
- 2 onions, chopped
- Garlic to your own tastes, chopped
- Whatever pumpkin you have
- Vegetable stock – I use bouillon, diluted in enough water to cover the solid ingredients
- 1-2 tsp. curry powder
- Salt and pepper to taste

Method

1   Melt the butter in a pan on a medium heat.

2   Add the cumin seeds. When they start to smell they are ready, usually after about 20 seconds. Take care not to burn them as it can make the soup bitter.

3   Reduce the heat and add the onions, then the garlic. Fry gently until translucent, about 5 minutes.

4   Add the pumpkin flesh and mix thoroughly to ensure it is coated with the butter. Fry for about 5 minutes, stirring frequently.

5   Add the stock, seasoning and curry powder, and bring to the boil.

6   Simmer for about 20 minutes or until the pumpkin is soft.

7   Blend into a smooth soup and serve, with a bit of cream if you are feeling indulgent.

TOASTED PUMPKIN SEEDS

These make a great quick snack and are full of nutrients and antioxidants, good for improved heart health, amongst other things. All you need to do is give them a rinse, allow to dry, season with salt, pepper and paprika, and toast in the oven for about 30 minutes, turning them every 10 minutes or so until they are golden.

November

As November settles in, so does the long winter darkness, making it even more important to get outside and capture what remains of the light. Focus is turning inwards, not just for us but also for the nature on our doorstep. By the end of the month, the last leaves, which have nobly clung to branches, will have let go, gracefully falling to the Earth to provide it with winter protection and spring nutrients. I love how trees put so much energy into growing new leaves in spring but are not afraid to release them when the time comes – a lesson for us all.

Many insects, birds and other animals become less visible, too, as the natural world slows down to almost a whisper. It's a good time for us to do the same, mindfully letting go of what has passed while being aware that spring will indeed come again. This month we will learn to accept this period of renewal, feel the liberation of letting go and prepare, not only for our future but for our children's and grandchildren's, too.

Make something and burn it

Having a bonfire on or around 5 November is a pretty normal thing for most of us living in the UK, as we celebrate the attempts made by Guy Fawkes to blow up the Houses of Parliament in 1605. Or do we celebrate him being caught? I'm never really sure. This year, have a mini fire in your own garden, or if you live in a flat then find a safe space outdoors, away from your or anybody else's property.

SUPPLIES

Willow and/or silver birch twigs

Flammable materials

Old tin camping plate or takeaway tin in which to seat fire, if needed

Here's how

1 It is a good time to harvest willow for weaving. You can find it growing in damp areas or by the side of a river. If you can't get hold of this then any flexible twigs will do, silver birch for example is a pretty common one.

2 Make some kind of vessel by weaving the twigs around each other. The best way to start is to make some kind of frame, a series of circles work well and then weave in between to join them together to form a sphere.

3 When it is complete stuff it with natural, flammable materials, like seed heads or thistle tops.

4 If you want, write down all of the things you would like to leave behind in your life on little bits of paper – bad habits, old thought patterns, self-destructive behaviours and so on – then push them into your vessel.

5 Add a bit of cotton wool for a little extra tinder to get it going. When you have finished your creation, go to your fire and burn it. If you don't have a fire pit then you can set it alight on an old metal camping plate or takeaway tin, though be careful to make sure that the ground below is not flammable.

6 Enjoy the satisfaction of spending hours making something and then watching it go up in flames; it reminds you to let go and to accept change, perfect for this time of year.

Scrumped apple pies

Scrumping or 'to scrump' means to steal orchard fruits, in Old English, and may have come from the word 'scrimp', meaning something that is dry and shrivelled up, not dissimilar to old windfall apples. I have many sources of locally grown apples, even in the inner city, and often people are happy for you to collect from their gardens if they have trees they don't use. So the word 'scrumping' takes on a slightly new meaning, which is actually doing people a favour by clearing up their unwanted fruit, rather than actually stealing it, which obviously I don't recommend.

It wouldn't be autumn without apples, or indeed without scrumping. There are around 2,500 varieties in the UK and they are a superfood in their own right. This year I decided to find a new way of enjoying them.

SUPPLIES

Pack of pre-rolled shortcrust pastry (you can make your own if you really want)

¼ apple per person

Caster sugar to taste

100g soft brown sugar

100g butter

200ml double cream

Dariole moulds, greased and lined, or bun or pie tins

Greaseproof paper

Baking beans

Here's how

1 On a lightly floured surface, cut the shortcrust pastry into small rounds and roughly line the dariole moulds. To stop the pastry from shrinking, ensure a bit of it comes over the edges of the moulds.

2 Weigh down the pastry with baking beans on a circle of greaseproof paper.

3 Bake in the oven at around 200°C for 15 minutes or until golden. Remove from the oven, tipping out the beans, then carefully tip the pastries out onto a cooling tray.

4 Peel, core, dice and stew the apples with a little water and sprinkle of sugar in a pan over a low heat until soft.

5 Meanwhile make the toffee sauce by melting the soft brown sugar, butter and cream in a clean pan, stirring until it no longer feels grainy.

6 Fill your apple pastries with stewed apple and drizzle liberally with the toffee sauce.

7 Enjoy but be careful, these will be hot.

Go on a night walk

A night walk begins at dusk, when the light is starting to fade and the day is just beginning to turn to night. Twilight refers to the time of day, whether morning or evening, where there is still light in the sky but the sun has dipped under, or has not yet risen, from the horizon.

There are three phases of twilight, named so that scientists and astronomers have a universal time for absolute dark. Civil twilight is the first, describing when the light begins to fade and the sun is just under the horizon, to 6 degrees below it. I like to think of this time as the time when people are coming home from work and being civil to each other over the garden wall. In nautical twilight, the next phase, most stars start to be visible and the sun is between 6 and 12 degrees below the horizon. Astronomical twilight is the last phase, just before true dark, when the sun is between 12 and 18 degrees below the horizon. Anything after that and it is officially dark, the time when stargazing can fully begin. Many people are afraid of being out in the dark, probably because our primary sense is sight (the brain has more areas to process vision than any of the other main senses), and this sense is greatly hindered in the darkness. If you can get over this, however, being out as darkness sets in is truly magical.

Here's how

1 Plan a route you know in the light, though everything looks different in the dark, and make sure you have plenty of warm clothes that are suited to the weather. Pack a warm snack and a drink if you wish.

2 Set off at dusk, trying to notice as the different stages of twilight pass. As you walk into the night you may want to find a place to sit and listen, remembering how quickly wildlife returns to an area once we are still.

3 To compensate for our limited sight, our other senses become more acute in the dark; noises that you hear seem louder than they did before, exaggerated by the fact that there are fewer sounds at night to compete with each other. Nocturnal animals rely on this, which is why they often have larger ears than daytime creatures. Make the most of this heightened sense and be aware of the things you can hear. Perhaps the birds are going to roost, often ending with crows and magpies, which chatter among themselves in the tree tops. After them, the night walkers come out. If you are lucky you may hear the 'twit' of a tawny owl, often followed by a 'twoo' from its mate, or the haunting cry of a city fox, admittedly a little spine-chilling if you don't know what to expect. You might notice the rustle of a hedgehog, now endangered in the UK, as it carries its 5,000 spines through the undergrowth looking for food; even the insects it hunts sound much bigger at night.

4 Hearing is not the only sense which works harder in the dark; our taste buds do too. In fact, I hear there is a restaurant in London that serves its meals under complete darkness to enhance the flavour of the food. If you have packed a warm snack, take your time in eating it, do you enjoy it more now than when it is light?

5 See the darkness come in, and walk for as long as you feel. If two minutes of full darkness is enough for you that is fine; if you want to walk all night there is nothing stopping you. Be sensible though: if like me you live in the city there will sadly be no-go areas after dark.

SUPPLIES
Clothes suitable for the conditions
Sit mat (optional)
Warm drink and snack (optional)

Plant a tree (even indoors)

Trees are the masters of all plants, and it is possible to enhance even the smallest of spaces by growing one. In a city environment they are essential; a large oak for example will store 1 tonne of carbon by its fortieth birthday, and every day in summer transpires 450 litres of water through its leaves and provides enough oxygen for four people. Modern architects are starting to recognise this, and are incorporating them into their urban landscapes, none more so than the Boeri Studio, who in 2014 finished the construction of the Bosco Verticale, or vertical forest, in Milan (right). This pair of high-rise residential tower blocks, hosts 800 trees, 5,000 shrubs and 11,000 flowering plants, which not only protect the residents from noise, weather and pollution but also convert almost 20 tonnes of carbon dioxide into oxygen every year.

You don't need that many to improve your landscape though; a single tree can absorb 4.5kg of particulate matter (air pollutants, including dust, pollen, soot and smoke) per year. A 2013 study by Lancaster University found that planting a row of silver birch trees on the street reduced the amount of particulates in residents' houses by 50 per cent. And it's not all about physical health either. Studies have found that trees in a school environment can improve behaviour and concentration, that trees viewed from hospital windows can reduce recovery time and the need for medication and have even shown that people who live on tree-lined streets are significantly less likely to be on medication for depression. Time to get planting.

Before you start, it is important to choose a tree that is suitable for your site. If you are intending to put one in a pot on your balcony, for example, then you need to make sure your balcony is strong enough, so choose a smaller tree which needs less soil. If you are planting in the ground then check your soil type first and be aware of other environmental aspects of your site, like sun, shade and wind level.

Consider your own needs from the tree and don't dismiss edibles, you can get a range of patio fruit trees suitable for even the smallest spaces these days. Look for local varieties, as they will grow better in your area.

If you have no available outdoor space at all then don't despair, there are plenty of house plants to choose from that will enhance your living space. Always make sure your selection reflects the plant's needs as well as your own; some like humidity and enjoy being in a bathroom, others need dry conditions and die if you overwater them. Some need regular attention, whereas others can cope with a good deal of neglect.

SUPPLIES
Spade or trowel, depending on tree
Your chosen tree
Pot and compost, if not planting in ground

Here's how

When it comes to planting, all trees have their own requirements, so it really depends on the one you choose as to how to plant it. Follow the label or ask the sellers to advise you on the best method. Generally speaking, though, it wants to be in the pot or ground to the same depth as it is currently planted. Stake it for at least the first couple of years and keep moist, especially if it is in a pot.

December

Whether you are a winter person or not, December is a time for sharing, a time to connect with other people, a time of togetherness. Many religions have festivals in this month and no surprise about that; we barely see any daylight, especially if we work indoors, and the need to bring in sparkle and friendship is greater than ever.

As always, try to get into the rhythm of the month and appreciate the natural cycle of the year; it's much better for your soul than fighting it, which will not make you anything other than miserable. To help maintain a positive mood, remember to count your blessings often, and spend as much time as you can catching the natural light, which is precious at this time of year.

This month we will be getting festive, enjoying Christmas crafting and spending time with others, sharing food and times outdoors.

Christmas wreath walk

A woodland walk in winter always reminds me of the cyclical nature of our planet. Though the natural world seems dormant at this time – and to be fair it has certainly slowed down – there is still plenty of life to observe. See how feathered Scandinavian visitors like redwings and fieldfares have arrived for winter respite, tip your hat to the snowdrops that are already starting to push up through the cold soil, or notice the young buds, which are sitting ready and waiting for the new year. It's an age-old tradition to bring greenery from the woodland to the house at this time and it helps you to connect with the life that is present, even in winter.

SUPPLIES

Decent pair of secateurs (I use floristry snips, which are great for all materials in this activity)

Copper wreath ring (can be bought inexpensively from the garden centre)

Some hay, straw or moss

Garden twine

Floristry wire, stout rather than fine

Greenery (see step 1 on p. 206)

Christmas ribbon

Gardening gloves (optional)

Pretty things like dried fruit slices, cinnamon sticks, pine cones, baubles or dried flowers

Wreath hanger to hang it over your door (available from garden centres)

People to walk with, if you're feeling sociable

Here's how

1 Go for a walk, preferably on a dry day, with a jute bag or basket and your secateurs. Collect things like holly, long strands of ivy and conifer fronds to bring back with you.

2 Make the wreath by laying a circle base material such as hay, straw or moss on a flat surface (traditionally moss is used and this does help to keep the greenery damp through the season, but I use straw because it's cheap and just as effective). Place the wreath ring on the circle of base material, then put another layer of base material on top.

3 Bind the materials together with garden twine, working round once in a clockwise direction, then crossing over, coming back on yourself anticlockwise, catching any loose bits of straw as you go.

4 To hide the base material, lay some of your collected conifer fronds on top and secure it with the twine in the same way as above. (Note this is not necessary if you have used moss.)

5 Attach your ribbon by folding it in half and pushing the fold through the top of the wreath, then push the two loose ends through the loop to make a lark's foot.

6 Cut your holly into short pieces, with a pointed stem to make them easier to stick into the base. Make sure that it is tucked in on an upward angle so it does not fall out when hung up. It can be useful to wear gardening gloves for this part, but try to find the thinner, rubber-gripped ones, so that you can still feel what you are doing.

7 Tuck one end of the ivy into the wreath and wrap it around the holly before tucking in the other loose ends.

8 To attach the pine cones, take a full-length piece of stout floristry wire and poke one end into the bottom open layer of the cone, hold it in place with your thumb and then wrap the rest full circle around the base of the pine cone. Take it over the starting point and then down into a point which you can push through the wreath and bend over on the back. Placed wisely, this can also help you to pin some of the holy down.

9 For fruit slices, take a piece of stout floristry wire, push the first inch through the fruit, bend it over and then pull it back on itself until it is secure. You can then use the longer end to push into the wreath, again bending the end into the back of the wreath.

10 To attach baubles, thread three on half a piece of stout floristry wire, then fold the shorter end back on itself to make a stem to push into the wreath.

11 Attaching dried flowers depends on the type; if it has a solid, large head then work in the same way as for dried fruit, if it has stems like a hydrangea then loop part of the wire over some of the stems and fold back on itself as with the baubles.

12 For cinnamon sticks just thread a piece of wire through the hole and twist together to form a pin.

13 With all of the attachments, once they are pushed through the wreath bend the wire and any sharp points back in on themselves so they do not scratch your door.

14 Hang the finished wreath using a special wreath hook, which leaves no marks behind. Stand back and admire your handiwork.

Bake bread on a skillet

It can be a little too cold to sit around outside without some form of heat at this time of year, and though a winter fire for cooking has similar requirements to a summer one – embers are best – it takes a little more preparation in winter. This is because it can be quite wet out, so collect or buy wood in advance and keep it nice and dry, ready for when you need it. I also prepare the bread dough at home in the kitchen so it has been kneaded in a clean environment, but this isn't essential.

SUPPLIES

Dry wood

Cast iron skillet (these can often be found in charity shops, also keep your eyes open at car boot sales and farm sales)

Packet of bread mix (I like a cheddar and sundried tomato one)

Winter vegetable soup or melted cheese (to eat with the bread)

People to share it with

Here's how

1 To get started, clear the fire pit of damp debris and build a raft of dry wood on the base; this will keep the young fire away from the wet ground, allow air flow and will contribute to the hot bed of embers as it burns.

2 Prepare plenty of small sticks, more than you think you will need. If the air is damp and cold it takes the fire longer to get going than it would in summer. If you are collecting the fuel from the woodland then look for dry standing dead wood, which snaps easily, this is often found in a hazel coppice if you have one nearby.

3 Lay the fire with an oxygen triangle (two sticks which cross each other at the top and are apart at the bottom, on which you place your tinder). This will help the fire get going, as you can lift the two open ends of the sticks, getting more oxygen into the fire.

4 Light the fire, keep an eye on it and keep feeding it with dry fuel. As a rule of thumb, don't add anything that is more than twice as big as the bits in the fire that are already burning.

5 Turn out the bread mix into the skillet and tilt it towards the fire, leaving it to rise a little, making sure you keep moving it around to catch the heat evenly. Note: the handle will be getting hot, so use heatproof gloves.

6 When you have enough embers, make a base out of two bigger logs and sit the skillet over some embers, place it on top and cook gently for about ten minutes or until the bread will move easily and the bottom is brown.

7 Turn the bread over and repeat on the other side, being sure to keep pulling a few embers between the logs to maintain heat.

8 Once the bread is brown on both sides and sounds hollow when you tap it, carefully remove from the heat and allow it to cool a little.

9 To serve the bread, rip a bit off and pass it around to dunk in winter vegetable soup, or melted cheese.

See a sunrise

I must say I am not a morning person. I'm far more likely to watch a sunset and stargaze with some good friends and a bottle of wine than get out of bed while it's still dark. However, at this time of year the sun rises pretty late in the UK, between 8:00 a.m. and 8:30 a.m., which makes it a bit easier to catch.

Sunrises are best viewed from a place of height, even if it's just from your kitchen window. Remember the sun rises in the south-east at this time of year, so you want to be able to see in that direction. As always, though, I think it's worth getting out, otherwise you will miss the crisp air, the light reflecting off the chimney pots and maybe even the odd car alarm, not the most relaxing of noises but part of being a resident of the city.

As you are getting out you might as well make an event out of it, which to me always means food. Over the page is an idea for a warming breakfast hash you can make up the night before and reheat in the morning and pop it in a food flask to keep it warm, just right for a solstice breakfast, to eat in or take away. Otherwise it is quick to make on the morning of the sunrise.

Food flask, bowl and spoon for
  outdoor eating

Crusty bread and butter

Olive oil for frying

1 large onion, finely diced

2 sweet potatoes, diced

1 red bell pepper, diced

250g mushrooms, chopped

1 tsp. paprika, or smoked paprika if
you prefer

1 tsp. cumin powder

½ tsp. red chilli powder

½ tsp. cinnamon powder

400g tin of chopped tomatoes

300g washed spinach

400g tin of butter beans, drained

Salt and pepper to taste

Here's how

1 Fry the onion in olive oil until translucent.

2 Add the sweet potatoes and cook until soft.

3 Add the red pepper and mushrooms, seasoning and spices and cook lightly, stirring often so it does not stick.

4 Pour in the tin of tomatoes and the spinach, mix well and cook for about ten minutes with the lid on, or until the vegetables are soft.

5 Add the butter beans and cook for a further five minutes, again with the lid on, so the beans can absorb the flavour.

6 In the morning, butter the crusty bread, reheat and spoon your food into a warm food flask.

7 Pack your breakfast and a warm drink and head out to watch the sunrise and welcome in light.

8 Spoon your warm breakfast hash onto the crusty bread, pour yourself a morning brew and enjoy.

Know when enough is enough

One of the things I respect about Scandinavian culture (not that I profess to know lots about it) is that they seem to look outwards, and are not as insular as we can be in the UK. Scandi culture has been slowly spreading to far corners of the world for many years. Their newest export is lagom, and it couldn't be a more appropriate post-Covid philosophy to take on board, especially at this time of year when excess dominates. It basically means not too little, not too much, just right, and if you haven't realised by now that having more just isn't cool, then you really need to prise yourself out of the 1980s and get with the programme.

If Covid taught us anything, then surely it's how important the people in our lives are and what precious sanctuary nature is.

So this festive season, let's celebrate the things that are really important, not compete for the biggest pile of pointless plastic under our Christmas trees.

Stop, breathe and know when enough is enough.

SUPPLIES
Soft lighting
Comforting food and drink
Blankets
Slippers

Here's how

1   It can be all too tempting to stay indoors to avoid the bad weather at this time of year but honestly, you will enjoy the warmth even more if you have made the effort to get out just for a little while.

2   Prepare your home in advance. If you have an open fire or wood burner then get it ready to light when you return.

3   If not you can achieve similar results with lighting. Choose low-watt light bulbs, pretty lights and candles (remember not to leave them unattended).

4   Prepare some rich food, bread, cakes, a good vat of soup and remember the drinks. Make a special hot chocolate with a nip of brandy, some fruity mulled wine or spiced apple juice.

5   Put out a basket of cosy blankets and tell people to bring their slippers, it's about comfort and a feeling of safety, not sequins and ballroom.

6   Now your home is ready, invite your friends for a walk, go out whatever the weather but be sensible, wear the right clothes and don't go as far if the weather is really bad and you are not used to it.

7   When you can start to feel the cold in your bones go home to the warmth, put the dinner in, soften the lighting, get comfy and enjoy some time with loved ones. Or just read a good book by the fire, listening to the wind and rain howling outside, while tucked up under a while blanket in your PJs. Winter bliss.

Winter wild weather activity:
Make an ice globe

With daylight hours at a minimum at this time of year, every bit of sparkle you can add to your life is a bonus, and the glass-like qualities of ice make it the perfect vessel for night lights.

OK, so we may not be at the standard of the ice sculptors of Harbin (though do check them out, they are amazing), but it's OK to allow your adult self to play from time to time. You don't have to be an expert in everything. Sometimes you can do things just because they're fun.

Here's how

1   Part fill three balloons with tap water.

2   Tie a knot in the ends.

3   Put balloons on a tray outside in the cold.

4   Leave until they are almost frozen, this can take a few hours or a few days, depending on the temperature. If the weather is not getting cold enough and you want to hurry them along a bit then you can put them in the freezer.

5   Keep checking them to make sure they do not freeze solid.

6   When they feel like they have a thick shell, remove the balloons and pour out the remaining unfrozen water.

7   Put a night light in the hole.

8   Enjoy.

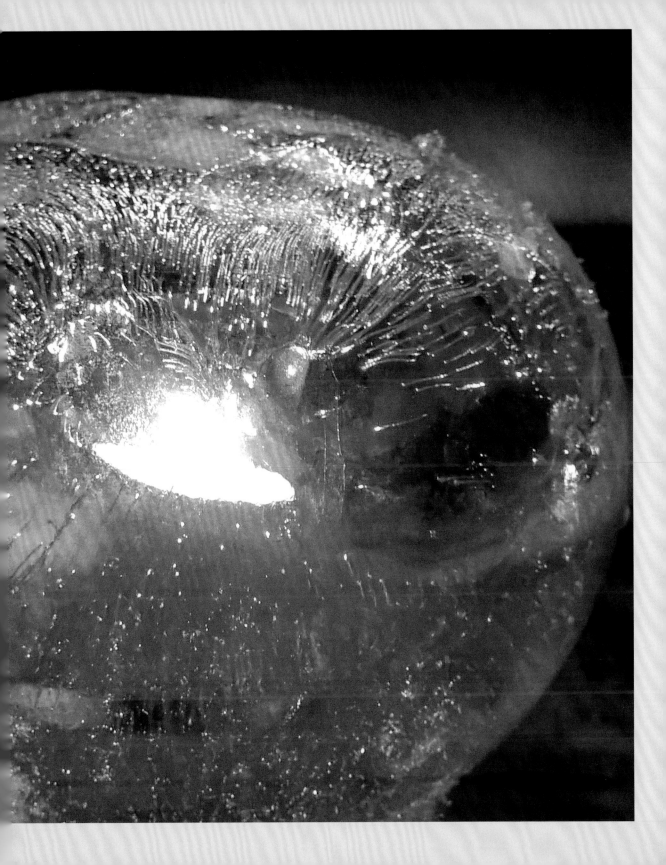

Further reading

Atkinson, C. (2015), *How to Make Your Own Cordials and Syrups*, London: Little, Brown

Baker, N. (2013), *RSPB Nature Tracker's Handbook*, London: Bloomsbury Publishing

Baker, N. (2017), *ReWild, the Art of Returning to Nature*, London: Aurum Press

Brown, K. (2014), *The Edible Flower Garden*, Leicester: Hermes House

Brown, R.W., Lawrence, M.J. and Pope, J. (2004), *Animals Tracks, Trails and Signs*, London: Hamlyn

Bruton-Seal, J. and Seal, M. (2008), *Hedgerow Medicine, Harvest and Make Your Own Herbal Remedies*, Ludlow: Merlin Unwin

Collard, P. (2014), *The Little Book of Mindfulness*, London: Gaia Books

Cornelius, G. (2005), *The Complete Guide to the Constellations*, London: Duncan Baird

Francis-Baker, T. (2021), *Concise Foraging Guide*, London: Bloomsbury Publishing

Francis-Baker, T. (2018), *Food You Can Forage*, London: Bloomsbury Publishing

Gooley, T. (2014), *The Walker's Guide to Outdoor Clues and Signs*, London: Sceptre

Jorgensen, P., ed. (2016), *Mocktails, Cordials, Infusions, Syrups, and More*, London: Ryland, Peters & Small

Juniper, T. (2013), *What has Nature Ever Done for Us? How Money Really Does Grow On Trees*, London: Profile Books

Launert, E. (1981), *The Country Life Guide to Edible and Medicinal Plants of Britain and Northern Europe*, London: Hamlyn

Li, Q. (2018), Shinrin-Yoku, *The Art and Science of Forest-Bathing*, London: Penguin

Mabey, R. (2012), *Food for Free*, London: Collins

Muir, L. (2017), *Wild Cocktails, from the Midnight Apothecary*, London: CICO Books

Nozedar, A. (2018), *Foraging With Kids*, London: Nourish

Patel, K. (2012), *Prashad, Indian Vegetarian Cooking*, London: Headline

Steel, S., ed. (2011), *Neal's Yard Remedies: Cook, Brew and Blend Your Own Herbs*, London: Dorling Kindersley

Warren, P. (2010), *101 Uses of Stinging Nettles*, Norwich: Wildeye

Wiking, M. (2016), *The Little Book of Hygge, The Danish Way to Live Well*, London: Penguin

Wild, A. and Pastor, C. (2019), *The Perfect Afternoon Tea Recipe Book*, Leicester: Lorenz Books

Yates, C. (2014) *Nightwalk: A Journey to the Heart of Nature*, London: William Collins

Resources

Air quality map
uk-air.defra.gov.uk/

Allotments application form
www.gov.uk/apply-allotment

Aromantic Natural Skin Care
www.aromantic.co.uk

Beaufort scale
www.metoffice.gov.uk/weather/guides/coast-and-sea/beaufort-scale

Cloud Appreciation Society
cloudappreciationsociety.org

DD Hammocks
www.ddhammocks.com/

G Baldwin & Co. for herbs, orris root and more
www.baldwins.co.uk

POMS questionnaire
www.topendsports.com/psychology/poms.htm

RNLI safe swimming advice
rnli.org/what-we-do/lifeguards-and-beaches

RSPB bird identifier
https://www.rspb.org.uk/birds-and-wildlife/wildlife-guides/identify-a-bird/

Woodland Trust find your nearest woods
www.woodlandtrust.org.uk/visiting-woods/find-woods/

Woodland Trust useful seasonal guide for wild edibles
www.woodlandtrust.org.uk/visiting-woods/things-to-do/foraging/

Image Credits

Bloomsbury Publishing would like to thank the following for providing photographs and for permission to reproduce copyright material within this book. While every effort has been made to trace and acknowledge all copyright holders, we would like to apologise for any errors or omissions, and invite readers to inform us so that corrections can be made in any future editions of the book.

With the exception of the photograph and image credits listed on this page, all photographs in *Urban Wild* were taken by the author and remain © Helen Rook.

1 both Nata Slavetskaya/Getty Images; 6-7 top row, left to right: Nata Slavetskaya/Getty Images; Elena Alfimova/Shutterstock; Nata Slavetskaya/Getty Images; 6-7 bottom row, left to right: Nata Slavetskaya/Getty Images; Nata Slavetskaya/Getty Images; Mecaleha/ Getty Images; Nata Slavetskaya/Getty Images; 13 Nata Slavetskaya/ Getty Images; 14 Nata Slavetskaya/Getty Images; 17 bottom Ace_ Create/Getty Images; 20 Olena Kravchenko/Shutterstock; 21 Gill Copeland/Shutterstock; 23 top Tim Large/Shutterstock; 23 bottom Nick Beer/Shutterstock; 24 top left Nata Slavetskaya/Getty Images; 24 top right Chamille White/Shutterstock; 24 bottom right Chamille White/Shutterstock; 25 bottom Albina Kosenko/Shutterstock; 26 Anna Aybetova/Shutterstock; 29 Nata Slavetskaya/Getty Images; 35 top right Ray Kennedy/rspb-images.com; 37 Jasmine Dadge; 38 top Dariana Oleinik/EyeEm/Getty Images; 38 bottom Cavan Images/Getty Images; 39 bottom Caroline Brady/EyeEm /Getty Images; 40 from top to bottom: Fafarumba/Shutterstock; ONYXprj/ Shutterstock; klreik78/Shutterstock; ONYXprj/Shutterstock; ONYXprj/Shutterstock; ONYXprj/Shutterstock; ONYXprj/ Shutterstock; 45 Lyona/Getty Images; 47 Nata Slavetskaya/Getty Images; 48 left TORWAISTUDIO/; 48 centre Eszter Ballo; 48 right Alex Ramsay/Alamy; 49 Eszter Ballo; 50 Eszter Ballo; 51 Sergio Photone/Shutterstock; 52 Nata Slavetskaya/Getty Images; 53 Stephen Rees/Shutterstock; 57 mecaleha/Getty Images; 59 Jacky Parker Photography/Getty Images; 61 top PJ photography/ Shutterstock; 63 top Daniela Baumann/Shutterstock; 63 bottom left HandmadePictures/Shutterstock; 63 bottom right DUSAN ZIDAR/Shutterstock; 64 right Roberto Castillo/Shutterstock; 65 Noel Powell/Shutterstock; 67 Nata Slavetskaya/Getty Images; 68 channarongsds/Getty Images; 69 top beats1/Shutterstock; 69 bottom left Ian Grainger/Shutterstock; 69 bottom right Jack N. Mohr/ Shutterstock; 71 Shokhina/Shutterstock; 72 bottom left AngieC333/ Shutterstock; 72 bottom right Julie Kamiya-Craig/Shutterstock; 75 wonderful-Earth.net/Alamy; 76 Elena Elfimova/Shutterstock; 79 Slavica Stajic/Shutterstock; 81 Ravsky/iStock; 82 top barmalini/ Shutterstock; 82 middle Sanny11/iStock; 82 bottom Wako Megumi/ iStock; 84 Aleksandra Duda/Shutterstock; 85 Nata Slavetskaya/Getty Images; 86 mecaleha/Getty Images; 87 top Lois GoBe/Shutterstock; 87 bottom right Esin Deniz/Shutterstock; 88 Nata Slavetskaya/ Getty Images; 90 Mabeline72/Shutterstock; 91 top Vronska/ Shutterstock; 91 bottom UVgreen/Shutterstock; 93 bottom tomertu/ Shutterstock; 94 Ola Tarakanova/Shutterstock; 99 top tbbstudio/ Shutterstock; 101 Nata Slavetskaya/Getty Images; 102 Uncle Leo/ Shutterstock; 103 bottom left Iva Vagnerova/Shutterstock; 107 top dragon_fang/Shutterstock; 107 bottom, Eszter Ballo; 113 Magdanatk /Shutterstock; 115 left Nitr/Shutterstock; 116 top right Alexandr Makarov/Shutterstock; 116 bottom right Kirill Aleksandrovich/ Shutterstock; 117 top AVN Photo Lab/Shutterstock; 117 middle spline_x/Shutterstock; 117 bottom joanna wnuk/Shutterstock; 119 Nata Slavetskaya/Getty Images; 120 R.Wilairat/Shutterstock; 121 top Paramonov Alexander/Shutterstock; 121 bottom left Leon Neal/Staff/Getty Images; 121 bottom right Education Images/ Contributor/Getty Images; 122 mansum008/iStock; 123 yasuspade/ Shutterstock; 124 Mazhar Khan Pathan/Shutterstock; 126 Volcko Mar/Shutterstock; 127 top Foxxy63/Shutterstock; 127 bottom left unpict/Shutterstock; 127 bottom right Sia Sia/Shutterstock; 129 top gpointstudio/Shutterstock; 129 bottom left Peter Etchells/ Shutterstock; 130 top and bottom AlinArt/Shutterstock; 131 top lovemydesigns/Shutterstock; 131 bottom Peg jet/Shutterstock; 132 Vladimir Wrangel/Shutterstock; 133 Nata Slavetskaya/Getty Images; 134 cornfield/Shutterstock; 135 top Peter Cripps/Shutterstock; 136 AlexMaster/Shutterstock 137 top PRESSLAB/Shutterstock; 137 bottom left cornfield/Shutterstock; 137 bottom right Michaelspb/ Shutterstock; 141, top tatishdesign/Shutterstock; 142 petroleum man/Shutterstock; 147 bottom right Eszter Ballo; 149 Nata Slavetskaya/Getty Images; 152 Galina Timofeeva/Getty Images; 154 Domareva.Tanya/Shutterstock; 155 Daria Fisun/Shutterstock; 157 top Steve JM Hamilton/Shutterstock; 160 AleksandraKuzmina/ Getty Images; 161 left callumrc/Shutterstock; 165 Nata Slavetskaya/ Getty Images; 167 top Peter Turner Photography/Shutterstock; 167 bottom left, Super 8/Shutterstock; 167 bottom right, Martin Fowler/Shutterstock; 169 top JoannaTkaczuk/Shutterstock; 169 bottom G.MARTYSHEVA/Shutterstock; 170–1 monkographic/ Shutterstock; 173 top Richard Griffin/Shutterstock; 173 bottom left Nadia Levinskaya/Shutterstock; 186 top Minur/Shutterstock; 188 xpixel/Shutterstock; 190 logaryphmic/Getty Images; 191 Mike A. Martin/Shutterstock; 192 PJ photography/Shutterstock; 193 top left Lizzie Lamont/Shutterstock; 193 top right edchechine/Shutterstock; 193 bottom Olga Razryadova/Shutterstock; 195 Raggedstone/ Shutterstock; 196 Nekrasov Eugene/Shutterstock; 197 top DRG Photography/Shutterstock; 198 Sabino Parente/Shutterstock; 199 top Dmytro Zinkevych/Shutterstock; 199 bottom panattar/Shutterstock; 201 ajlatan/Shutterstock; 202 olga che/Shutterstock; 203 Nata Slavetskaya/Getty Images; 204 Slavetskaya/Getty Images; 206 Tatyana Soares/Shutterstock; 215 Javen/Shutterstock; 217 kryzhov/ Shutterstock.

Index